BEIJING BLUR

"Poignant and revelatory" *Adelaide Advertiser*

"West's voice rings with insight" *Courier Mail, Brisbane*

"What West has done is explore the Chinas you never hear of, or those whose existence the reader may even have assumed impossible... intimate, evocative and erudite writing, shimmering with honesty" *Canberra Times*

"You'll be swept up in the energy, contradiction and confusion that is modern Beijing" *The Cairns Post*

"Bang on target" *Sunday Age, Melbourne*

"The best travel writers come across as afable companions who balance fact with entertainment and West has it down" *Madison Magazine*

"Fascinating and intimate" *Q News*

James West is a young Australian writer and radio broadcaster who worked as a 'Foreign Expert' in Beijing from 2005 to 2006. After completing a master's in journalism at New York University, he returned to Australia, where he is executive producer of current affairs programme, *Hack* on ABC radio. He lives in Sydney.

BEIJING BLUR

A head-spinning journey into modern China

JAMES WEST

crimson

Author's note

Some names and identifying descriptions in *Beijing Blur* have been changed.

This edition first published in Great Britain 2009 by
Crimson Publishing, a division of Crimson Business Ltd
Westminster House
Kew Road
Richmond
Surrey
TW9 2ND

First published by Penguin Group (Australia), a division of Pearson Australia
Group Pty Ltd, 2008

A catalogue record for this book is available from the British Library.

ISBN 978 1 85458 468 7

Printed and bound by Mega Printing, Turkey

CONTENTS

For Nick

PART ONE

SUMMER

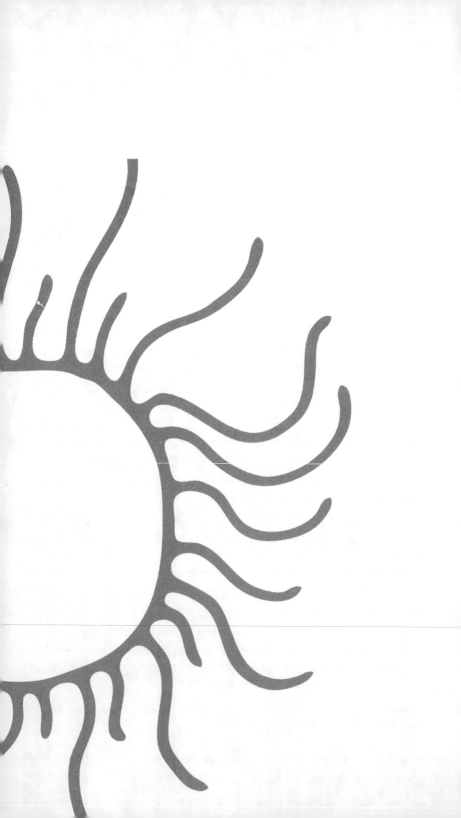

CHAPTER 1

GREAT WALL RAVING

'We are the wall!' they screamed. 'Bring down the wall!'

The last horde this loud hailed from fourteenth-century Mongolia; their weapon of choice sturdier than a glow-stick.

Beijing's own MCs Raph and Webber – buzz-cut prophets in low-slung jeans – led the heaving mob, accompanied by a guy called Elemental from New Zealand on decks and Powerbook.

Raph was as light and deadly as a boxer. His contorted face spat unbroken Chinese. His wet shirt clung to his skinny frame. Behind him, a VJ projected images of Beijing's ubiquitous cranes cut with vintage Bruce Lee onto the Great Wall. Green laser tracings splintered through brick turrets like arrows.

A Chinese girl with glitter makeup, a baggy Velvet Underground t-shirt and a lollipop flicked me a grin. 'Do you know the only phrase in Chinese you need? *Sui bian!* Whatever!' She took my hand. 'Whatever!'

I looked up to see our collective steam rise and seep into the moonlit valley. Then, in a mad rush of vodka to my 3 a.m. brain, it hit me. China! There was no mention of the booming economy, the death of the Mao suit, pan-Asian free trade agreements and billion-buck uranium deals. It was my first Saturday night in Beijing.

I was dancing on the Great Wall of China.

Two days before, I had needed a friend.

In my journal was the number for an old workmate's drinking buddy who now lived in Beijing. *Stephen*. An Australian. I gave him a call.

We agreed to meet in Wudaokou in the Haidian district of north-western Beijing that Saturday. The 'Wu' was home to several of the big universities including Tsinghua, Bei Da – better known in the West as Peking University – and Beijing Language and Culture University, where Stephen studied Chinese full-time.

In the Wu, student demographics skewed towards modish South Koreans on a year abroad. There were also horny American college kids emancipated from parents, arty French chicks and the odd Iranian or Uzbek on an embassy internship.

The district had plenty of good Korean barbecue joints, and Propaganda Bar, the city's most efficient meat market, was packed every night of the week with over-styled youngsters in ripped mesh tops, Chinese hip-hoppers in cornrows, flirty waiters on whose cheekbones you could slice and dice basically anything.

In the centre of this mini-Seoul was Lush, a café-bar above a bookshop near the lightrail station. An English menu with lasagne, focaccia and imported beers, the couches, Wi-Fi and open-mic nights on Sundays drew loyal crowds. The downside was its sceney mix of DJs and their insipid acolytes. Party polaroids of the clique were taped to the walls.

The Great Wall rave buses were about to leave from outside Lush when a foreigner entered shaking hands and kissing cheeks. He was wearing a red McDeath book bag, cords with a slight flare and a red t-shirt with a target in the centre. Bullseye.

'Stephen!' I called. 'Hey!' I pushed through the crowd with contemporary East Asian haircuts, long at the back and anime-sculpted along the sides. This city had great hair. Every second shop was a hairdressers, over-staffed by sexy cutters till late, seven days a week. Stephen's own hair was full, sandy brown and messy like he'd just woken up.

'G'day. Shit, sorry. I've forgotten your name.' Stephen said. 'I just woke up.'

'No worries. It must be weird, a phone call out of the blue like that. James.' We shook hands. 'Glad this is on. Thanks for letting me know. I was feeling like I needed to hear some English.'

'Of course. But you're having a dream run. First weekend and you're off to a rave on the Great Wall. Now, let's get supplies.'

Supplies for the three-hour bus ride included Chinese Red Bull, local beers and chips from the busy corner store.

'So why have you come to this crazy place?' Stephen asked when we got comfortable on the bus. He opened a longneck of Tsingtao and handed it over.

'I'm here for twelve months,' I took a swig. The beer tasted clean and metallic. 'Working for state-run radio.'

His eyes went wide. 'Full on. Doing what?'

'Polishing scripts for the English-language service. My first day is tomorrow.'

'How on earth did an 18-year-old land that gig?'

'I'm 23, actually.' It was a familiar taunt. 'The ABC sent me over from Sydney. It's an exchange. Someone here went to Melbourne for the ABC's Mandarin service. This is the second year of the programme.'

'At China Radio International, right?' asked Stephen. I nodded. 'I hear it's huge and kinda scary.'

'They say its like China's CNN or BBC. There are bureaus every-where, but someone told me that the correspondent in DC isn't allowed into the White House.'

'Doesn't surprise me one bit,' said Stephen.

'And how old are you?' I asked. I figured about 32.

Stephen had just turned 40 but said he often lied about his age, especially to girls in Wu cafés from whom he needed tricky Chinese-language advice. He had an unlined face in neat propor-tions and steel-blue eyes, a beachy Baldwin without the height (he was about 5ft 6in tall).

Even after his fortieth – a coming out – disbelief remained. 'But he acts so young,' they would say.

I put it down to all-afternoon sleeping, what I would later call 'grandpa naps', where he would turn off his mobile phone and be uncontactable.

Outside the bus it was raining. We were now free of the city on a multi-lane carriageway and heading northeast. Apart from several floodlit petrol stations big enough to refuel jets, our surroundings were hard to make out; the road was fast and dark.

'How's learning Chinese?' I asked Stephen as we were arriving at the wall.

'If it's not bloody painful, then you're not learning Chinese,' he laughed, and the gang around us, mostly students, agreed.

'You need to know over three thousand characters to read the newspaper,' the New Zealand boy behind us despaired. 'Three thousand!'

'And there are so many measure words,' a South African girl chimed in.

'What are they?' I asked, wondering how much pain I was in for.

'Those extra words you use with numbers when you're counting things out,' another girl explained. 'Like two pairs of trousers, or five head of cattle. There are heaps more in Chinese than in English.'

'But I reckon once you get your head around four tones, wacky grammar and the Beijing accent, you'll be just fine,' Stephen winked.

'Right,' I said. Shit, this was going to be difficult.

'It's fun. But start learning as soon as you can. I'll be badgering you if you don't,' he said. 'Deal?'

'Deal.'

The rave was held at the Jinshanling section of the wall, about 120 kilometres from Beijing in neighbouring Hebei province. In Hebei, organisers could stage events on the wall to raise money for its upkeep. At Badaling, the touristier showcase closer to Beijing, this wasn't allowed for heritage reasons, even though authorities had said yes to a Starbucks and a KFC.

'How fucking cool is this, man?' Stephen said when we first spotted the world's longest manmade structure.

I was gobsmacked. 'That's one ridiculous wall,' I sighed. We stood and gazed at the wall flop and rise like an ancient rollercoaster.

'A third of the Chinese population at the time built it,' Stephen said. From the base of the mountain, the brick defences reared up and marched across the ridges into the night.

'They don't do things by halves, do they? Why on earth would you build this thing?' I said.

He didn't answer my question. Instead, his response was, 'We *have* to get some drugs.'

The party was split across two areas. The first was the natural stage at the base of one of the mountains, with the battlements looming a few hundred metres above. Here DJs Dio and Mickey Zhang played techno and trance with drug-happy crescendos that had dancers leaping for joy and gripping each other when the tension broke into a more consistent heart-thumping beat.

For the more adventurous raver, a thin trail wound around the sides of the first stage and up a series of steep footpaths to the crumbling garrisons of the wall itself. Cherry-flavoured vodka was served from big plastic barrels and the music was a mixture of foreign-language hip-hop, funky house and Chinese rap, which later evolved into endless break-beats and slick drum-and-bass for those who had kissed sleep goodbye for the next week.

I wanted to meet as many people as possible, and was suddenly swamped by interesting folk. I got stoned with a group of Norwegian students behind the lighting truck, where we giggled about toilets and danced in a circle. I met lots of Chinese university students. One girl in the dancing crowd on the lower tier tried to kiss me, but I slipped back into the throng.

On the way to find Stephen I met Jason. He appeared to be by himself so I said hello and we struck up a conversation.

'Are you wearing makeup?' I asked.

'No, I'm not,' he lied. A line of dark makeup down the bridge of his nose gave him an angular, predatory look. His skin was flawless brown. He was pierced several times down each ear and once just below his bottom lip. His head was shaved, which made his almost-black eyes look bigger.

Jason had spent some time in New Zealand but was back in Beijing trying to find more work. His family was from Harbin, in the chilly northeast of China, and he balanced a budding music career with work in advertising and modelling. He also wanted to be an architect. He was 22 and was already getting sick of Beijing. He wore a t-shirt with Rolling Stones-style red lips on its front.

I told him about how in two days I had a meeting with an estate agent to look at a converted traditional courtyard house near Tiananmen Square. It was near the subway that would take me out west to work without having to change lines.

'I could come and help you with language so they don't rip you off,' he offered. 'Why don't we make a day of it and go to IKEA and get you some stuff?'

'Only if you have time,' I said.

'Sure. I work at night. It could be fun,' he smiled.

'Exactly what I need, man. Thanks. I didn't know there was an IKEA here,' I said. Relief. IKEA, and someone to take me there. Apparently, Beijing has the biggest IKEA outside of Stockholm. Something to do with the new middle class having more disposable income.

'Funny,' said Jason, 'I went to an IKEA in New Zealand and there were lots of photos of families with four or five members. Here there are pictures of only one child. And they don't sell bunk beds.'

I laughed. 'You don't have siblings?'

'No one does, James. My friends are my brothers and sisters.'

We exchanged numbers – I had bought a mobile phone the day before. 'Hey, you look like that guy from *Lord of the Rings*, what's his name? Frodo! You look like Frodo,' he said.

'Oh no,' I groaned. 'Not you too.' Everyone in China seemed to think I looked like Frodo.

'See ya, Mister Frodo.' He stuck his tongue out.

I found Stephen in the main turret of the wall chatting to two criminally attractive young Koreans.

Perched in a broken fortress, Stephen and I drank Tsingtao as dawn broke across Jinshanling. A spectacle of light; the sky's royal blue softened with pinks. The wall's shadow lost ground to the green of shrubbery. Then Stephen and I walked along the wall for an hour. I listened to the hum of insects and smelled rich Chinese soil for the first time. A foreigner and a Chinese girl groped in a grotto. I stepped over a used condom. The wall sat in the morning haze like a sleeping snake.

'I can't believe you have to work today, man,' Stephen said when we got back on the bus at 7 a.m.

'I wouldn't have missed that for the world,' I replied. 'I'm in China. Only last week I was saying goodbye and quitting my job. This is unbelievable.'

'Good to meet you, James.' He drifted off to sleep as flat farmland slipped by.

I felt as if I'd known Stephen forever.

As for Jason, I pulled out my phone and texted: 'Dinner tomorrow night?' Then, recklessly: 'I'm drunk enough to say I think you are cute. I hope that doesn't make things weird.'

His beeping response was the only sound on the sleeping bus. 'Ha. Well, I'm glad we cleared that up. Likewise. Dinner would be great. Sleep well.'

One night. A best mate and a date.

CHAPTER 2

I SEE RED

When coal burns, carbon dioxide is released. It reacts with nitrogen in the air to form nitrogen oxides that accumulate into reddish-brown chemical clouds, not unlike the one my plane pushed through above Beijing.

The plane's wing lights made the pall blink green. Then I saw the orange city, made more luminous by scattered late-afternoon light. By the time we had landed on the tarmac, whole spectra had been rubbed out. The sepia haze was inside the terminal. I squinted to make out the baggage turnstiles. The accompanying smell of bad eggs and chemical effluent was robust and sour.

Bu, a smiling, fussy man in an open-necked shirt and black slacks, had met me at Beijing Capital Airport that previous week. He first pushed a security pass into my hand then shook it, as if cementing a secret accord. 'Welcome, welcome, James. You look so young!' he giggled. 'This way.'

Bu worked at China Radio International, China's biggest radio station and my new workplace. He led me through the car park to an idling black sedan with its lights on. A driver waited inside. I sat in the back and put my bags down. Bu shut the door behind me so that for a moment I was left with the large, silent form of the driver.

'Workers in the English service,' Bu was saying, 'they work very hard, you know, very long hours, in at work every day.' He hopped into the passenger seat. The ding of the seatbelt reminder sounded on and on without acknowledgement from either Bu or the driver.

Bu laughed a repetitive, friendly laugh and began some flight chitchat as we slid out of the airport and down the expressway into the city. The laugh seemed to convey most of what went unsaid, which was, *Welcome to Beijing, kiddo. You have no idea what you're in for.*

I was in China and I wanted something more Chinese than Chinese: bigger, better, badder, redder.

I had a grab bag of expectations from growing up. My first experience of China was the suburban Chinese restaurant. As a kid, it was the Golden Dragon (that might not have been its real name, but it sums up the various Chinese restaurants of the time), which had large tanks full of fish destined for the table. When we dined in, we asked for cutlery, and sharing was made easy by a greasy lazy Susan. At home in front of *Hey Hey It's Saturday* we formed opinions about the food's quality: the sweet and sour pork was too oily, there wasn't enough meat in the sang choy bow. Menus were demoted down the stack kept next to the phone. Chinese was shorthand for relaxation – it meant a break for Mum, and leftovers were frozen, reheated and served on toast for a week.

On nights before going to the cinema, we headed to Dixon Street and the Hingara, where the staff never changed and the Laminex tables were scuffed right back to the underlying chipboard. The tangled streets of Sydney's Chinatown, dark with hanging meat and shadowy doorways, were exciting. It was slumming with good food, and we were treated like little princes.

China also became increasingly present in the suburbs. My brother and I swear that one day our parents told us to keep the dogs away from the front fence because the family across the road liked to eat dog.

I knew China through the stereotypes Australians had given its immigrants: Chinese people can't drive; they live to work, they don't work to live. The girls are shy and keep to themselves; the boys can be girly but are good at maths (we called them 'tech heads').

There were dozens of Chinese girls whose names I didn't know at high school. That had seemed OK. Now I wanted to go back and ask them, 'Where does your family come from? What do your parents do? How did you get here?'

At the turn of the millennium there were over half a million people living in Australia with Chinese ancestry, including families of the 42,000 students Prime Minister Bob Hawke gave residency to in the aftermath of the 1989 Tiananmen Square protests, the biggest influx of Chinese since the gold rush of the 1850s. Chinese-Australians became prominent in Australian public life. A parliamentarian or two, a famous heart surgeon, a newsreader and those that aced high-school finals – these were the Chinese who had made it into mainstream Australia, and into my expectations of what I would find.

China also held the promise of dragons' heads, acrobatics, brothels, mahjong, shouting waiters and women bailing water out of shopfronts. That was the Asia I'd seen in Hong Kong films: all wide angles, drenched in colour. It wasn't kung-fu films or Chinese period dramas that resonated with me – every country has its historical pantomime. *Contemporary* Asia, however, had me transfixed.

Wong Kar-Wai's *2046*, set in the Oriental Hotel, depicts an Asia full of glistening streets, elegant chaos, and sultry, perpetual night (handy to make use of cities flooded in neon). A political note sounds under the film. The year 2046 will mark fifty years since the handover of Hong Kong back to China from British rule, the fifty years under the 'One Country, Two Systems' promise. 'Well, that's a very interesting promise,' said Wong Kar-Wai in one interview with the ABC, 'so I wanted to make a film about promise.' The promise that love will last the passage of time, the promise that Hong Kong's soul will stay the same. His film had left me with an impression of China's mystery, its threat and its power.

Because I didn't know any better, all Asian countries and cities promised this Asia *noir*. I was also expecting, alongside this street-level stuff, a display of kitsch, old-school communism: messages daubed on walls, Mao sculptures propped up against cash registers, crumbling socialist monoliths.

But when my eyes hit Beijing for the first time from the back of Bu's car, all this fell away. There were no beauties scampering down streets with umbrellas. No Chinese Clark Gables smoking in doorways. Instead there was a loud, dirty, busy city made all the more blurry at 120 kilometres per hour. I tugged on my seatbelt and the driver's eyes met mine in the rear-view mirror. I let the belt retract as if simply testing the smoothness of the apparatus. The driver hadn't said a word and he wasn't going to.

Beijing looked like a city in a children's book, or the city your parents warned you about. There were dark structures and streets flying off in all directions. 'I bet it will look alien, like the landscape of another planet,' a friend's voice came to me. But then it didn't seem alien; it was, in fact, just the opposite – bleakly generic, leaving me suddenly without traction. I felt like I was going backwards and downwards to somewhere very dark.

The city's most noticeable feature was its construction scars. This, I learned later, was probably the most Chinese thing about Beijing.

Size was next. We'd been driving for a long time. My eyes soared along the scores of apartment blocks that lined the East Third Ring Road. They looked derelict but were teeming with life. *Somewhere in there*, I thought, passing windows germinating with light, *somewhere there are people I will meet, people I will eventually befriend, admire, dislike, even hate. I wonder what they're doing now. I wonder who they will be. In a country with 200 million young people, it shouldn't be too hard, should it?* I tried to imagine walking these streets once they were familiar. *Somewhere in among all these buildings I will find places to eat, I will learn another language, I will get very drunk, I'll feel elation and loneliness and more, I'll feel the daily grind of work and of life.* I closed my eyes as the feeling of everything that *wasn't yet* washed over me.

Bu and I finally talked about China Radio International. He told me about the radio station's new security checkpoints. An Australian, he said, recently got into a skirmish with guards at the first checkpoint for riding his bike into the complex without displaying his ID. Several soldiers from the People's Liberation Army ran at him wielding batons and tackled him to the ground, bike and all. The Australian grabbed one of the military officers by the jacket and shoved him away, scattering the other PLA soldiers.

'He does work there though, right?' I asked.

'Very serious,' said Bu, shaking his head.

'But he works there?'

'Yes . . . of course. You'll meet him,' Bu replied.

I was impressed. Real life-sized PLA soldiers sounded too exciting to be true.

It was dark now. We pulled off the road to stop abruptly in front of a decorative hotel facade with storey-high letters: Beijing Friendship Hotel. Red-spotlit conifers and hedges lined the driveway. Dragons licked their lips, looking ready to leap from awnings.

The silent driver popped the boot. Bu grabbed my pack, eager to bundle me inside.

A sour-faced receptionist in a red suit gave me the keys. No eye contact. She made me sign my name three times, stamped a few documents in red and made a dozen photocopies of my passport.

I was in a hotel the size of a suburb; an apartment as extensive as my house and backyard in Sydney. A central hallway led into a living area with a television, phone, desk and 1970s-era couches. The bedroom had two single beds, a dresser, a tallboy and a wardrobe. There was a flask of hot water and a tray of teas. How could a city of 15 million people feel this empty? A red glow suffused the place. I put down my pack and looked around to see Bu's hand still on the doorknob.

'I'm going now,' he said. He shut the door behind him and I never saw him again.

I stood for a moment in the hallway stretching my sore back, then ran the bathroom tap to splash my face. In the mirror, I noticed my eyes were bloodshot. Everything else was in order: spiky dark hair, pale skin with heavy eyebrows, small mouth. What little stubble I could grow was all-present. I wondered how much my face would change in a year. My stomach crested a wave of loneliness and I suddenly felt sick. I breathed in to steady myself and turned off the tap.

'Right,' I said aloud and my mouth hardened into a determined smile. I switched off the light and got ready for bed.

The Friendship Hotel was once the largest garden-style hotel in Asia. Its buildings spread across a 335,000-square-metre estate – 150 football fields of pure hotel. It was built by the Russians as a hotel for visiting communist consultants just five years after the People's Republic was founded. It still retains a sense, albeit faded, of political importance in its winding wings, the thirty-eight meeting rooms (with XL-sized tapestries of the Great Wall), tiered gardens, waterfalls and pagodas.

It had served another purpose too. Nearly three decades ago, the senior female staff at the Friendship Hotel were said to be prostitutes who had been rehabilitated after the Communist Revolution. At that time, there were four types of foreigner in Beijing. There were the students in the dormitories across the north's Haidian district, who by law had to lay low on campus, though some sneaked off to live with their Chinese boyfriends and girlfriends illegally in labyrinthine apartments. There were the journalists, including ABC correspondents, who lived under surveillance in diplomatic compounds around Jianguomen in the central embassy district, alongside the third type of foreigner, the diplomat.

One of the more famous diplomatic families to spend time in Beijing was the Bush family. In his late 20s, George W Bush, on vacation from Harvard, hung around Beijing for two months while his dad was US Chief Liaison Officer. Bush Snr was in the capital from 1974–1975, appointed by President Ford before the establishment of official diplomacy. In his journal, Bush Snr, aged 50, wrote, 'George will have a great time hitting [the ball] with the Chinese in both ping pong and tennis.'

George Jnr's formative experiences in Beijing were later confirmed for me by Jerome Cohen, current Professor of Law at New York University and a man who had played an advisory role in normalising relations between the USA and China. 'He rode around on a bicycle, looking for women,' Cohen joked after a speaking engagement in New York. 'Perhaps that's why he hasn't messed up our China policy like he's messed up just about everything else!'

The final type of foreigner in those days was the Foreign Expert, a breed of international hippy either on a lark or indulging an obsession with the East. This type comprised Sinophiles, academics working in language departments of universities, engineers or other skilled professionals from places as far flung as Iran, Albania and Central Africa, as well as Australians. These experts shacked up together in the Friendship Hotel.

There was a glamour about the place then because there was nowhere else for these foreigners to stay. Back then, there were only about 100 foreigners in the city. One Australian, Bruce Doar, an academic from the Australian National University, lived in the Friendship for over ten years, eventually taking over two of the larger apartments. Bruce – theatrical and brilliant – held parties in his rooms that lasted for weeks.

'I've never lived in a boarding house,' Bruce told me later, 'but I can imagine a boarding house might come close to the Friendship Hotel. It was barbarous, a jungle really. Relationships didn't survive.'

Bruce spoke of bodies strewn in corridors and regular excursions to the hospital by ambulance. 'It was demented but exciting, in many ways much more exciting than today. It was like all the foreigners had been put together so they would eventually tear each other apart with hysterical behaviour. The oppressive nature of the Chinese authorities had that effect.'

Coded messages were taped to the doors of apartments indicating the room numbers of the following weekend's parties. Unlike the Jianguomen compounds, the Friendship was patrolled less often, and students and local Chinese visited at night without too much fuss.

The Friendship's rooftop beer garden was the place to drink Tsingtao and compare battle wounds from a day out in the Wild East. According to Bruce, 'It was an alcoholism-creation zone.'

In 1989 a different kind of friendship was extended at the hotel. After the Tiananmen Square massacre, some of the foreigners in the Friendship offered their quarters as safe houses; the rehabilitated prostitutes didn't tell. The majority of the population opposed what happened in the square, and the hotel turned a blind eye – better for dissidents to be sheltered by foreigners than by Chinese, which could have meant reprisals.

During the early 1990s there were rumours that CRI and other organisations were receiving hefty kickbacks for housing Foreign Experts at the hotel, pocketing a significant part of the government subsidy they received per employee. Finally, around 1995, the experts were allowed to leave the Friendship and live in the real Beijing. Despite its illustrious expat history, the Friendship's time had passed.

By 2005, according to the Chinese Ministry of Labour and Social Security, I was one of 150,000 foreigners legally employed in China, a figure that had doubled in three years. About 1,000 Australians were officially registered with the Australian Embassy as expats in the capital, though they claim there were possibly another 1,000 who weren't. Americans made up the lion's share of foreigners, with some 40,000 citizens in the capital at any one time.

By the time I reached the lifeless Friendship there was only a handful of long-termers left. Much of the hotel was under refurbishment, including, to my regret, the 50-metre outdoor swimming pool. I was living in a relic.

After only a few days there I became obsessed with getting out.

I was stuck between cultures, buffered by people who had to be nice to me. My bed was made, my clothes folded and a new flask of hot water filled and ready at my door with a copy of the *China Daily* when I returned. I needed chopsticks and a wok. I was spending money like (bottled) water. And without a working knowledge of bus and tram routes, the Friendship was too far from the city centre, where the chance of meeting people increased with the number of Tsingtaos.

There was an added incentive to move out. Housing and transport would be subsidised by CRI to the tune of 7,000 RMB per month (over £550) as soon as I rented somewhere.

I began spamming classifieds websites, then waited for replies.

CHAPTER 3

SANG NA TIAN

I am lying next to Nick. It's a few days before I leave Sydney. We are hugging. To be in bed with Nick is to hug, it's always been that way when we sleep, like it has been for the last two and a half years. There is no prescribed role in the hugging, no spooner or spoonee. Neither of us provides something the other can't. It's a revolving thing. As long as most of our bodies are touching most of the time we are OK. It is ritual, an unquestioned thing, and we remain locked that way until morning, when our bodies again find independence.

But tonight there's no sleep. Tonight an alarm has been triggered at a big house across the road, a rapid wailing, rising and falling, ceaseless.

Outside Nick's window, apartment blocks are lit up, creating pale orange boxes of mosaic light. We can see the fireflies of lit cigarettes on balconies, people watching the blue butterfly shadows of a television in a dark room, or people like us, in bed, watching and waiting for the owner to be contacted and the noise to stop. The neighbourhood is awake in the still winter night. Maybe they're hugging too. I've never been awake with this many people before, in the dead of night. There's something I feel I belong to, something that feels like home.

'I'm scared,' I tell Nick. And I am. The Germans have a name for this emotion, this intense panic, this bewildering array of ups and downs. They call it *torschlusspanik*, the panic of the closing of the doors. For the last few weeks I have stayed with Nick. I have never lived with a boyfriend before and I feel closer to him than ever before. I finally feel like a grown-up.

'It's exciting though. We're too young, you need to see the world,' Nick says quietly, eyes shut. 'It would be silly for me to ask you to stay. You need to do this.'

I start to cry into his chest. 'Why am I doing this to you? I feel like the worst person in the world. If I can give you up, what else am I capable of?'

'Great things, bub. You get to work in China. And we get to talk every night.'

I feel paralysed. The siren wails. I am so sad.

'I'll miss you so much,' I say, and grip him tighter. 'So fucking much.' Each time I grip him it makes it more painful and I want to cry more. Nick strokes my hair.

We lie awake for two more hours, gently shifting into different hugs, me touching my favourite part of his body: the bit where his chest turns into his shoulder.

'You'll always be mine,' he whispers. 'I don't think many other people would put up with me but you, and you're mine.'

At 4 a.m. we hear a car pull up outside the big house, and a roller door creak open. We pull ourselves to the window to watch the finale. People are out on their balconies and at windows, fuzzy silhouettes staring, shell-shocked.

Suddenly the world tingles and races with silence. 'Finally, you fucker,' one guy shouts down from an apartment building. The silence ripples through the air like cool water, I can feel it touch my face and caress the inside of my head. Silence has never been this audible.

Slowly the mosaic loses its orange tiles, one by one, and TVs are switched off. People pull curtains, turn over and switch off bedside lamps, rearrange the bedcovers, and humph down to sleep for what is left of the night.

Nick and I wake up late to the bright sunlight feeling hungover, but as if something momentous has occurred. We shower. We don't talk much that day but we smile. And I pack the last of my things.

The Chinese call it *sang na tian* – sauna weather. It was a searing heatwave. Temperatures topped 40°C every day. I could feel the Gobi Desert creep closer. (It is moving to Beijing at a rate of two kilometres a year.)

On my second day I had a simple plan: to get to Tiananmen Square.

I was wet the second I left my hotel room. The air was heavy with pollution. The sun looked like a satellite in a dying solar system.

The street was a frenzy of activity. There were dumpling sellers huddling over towers of steam, t-shirt touts clapping hands, megaphone-wielding magazine hawkers, couriers on scooters shouting into mobile phones and students from nearby Remnin University moving like a single swarm of bees. There were rickshaw drivers, spitting old men whose shirts were hiked above their bellies, women with makeup sliding over their faces. Cars, cars, cars, and the rampant din of horns.

I boarded the subway. The sweltering heat steamed up the carriage windows. I was gang-pressed against one hundred fleshy forearms. Those lucky enough to get a seat copped the worst of the condensation; those standing were watered by overhead fans acting like backyard sprinklers.

After studying the map and working out my route, I looked down to see a cute baby sitting on his mother's lap. He was wearing those eminently practical trousers with the gusset cut out, everything on display.

The kid pissed all over my jeans. I hollered. The mother blinked then redirected his penis to the floor of the carriage. The piss went all over my shoes before spraying a businessman's briefcase. The plastic carrier bags of a handful of senior citizens caught the warm splashback. The businessman with the briefcase winked at the mother, while the grandmothers cooed and whistled at the culprit, pressing snacks of dried raisins into his mother's handbag.

The combination of ammonia, body odour and heat made me swoon. Piss ran the length of the carriage, under grocery bags and patent-leather shoes.

I gargled and tried to push my way to the other side, attracting indignant stares from my fellow commuters. *Stupid Westerner*, one look said. *Thinks he's better than us. Making all that fuss over some kid.* I panicked and kept pushing. For the final four stops I was pinned by passive, unnerving stares.

Only much later, well after the second time I was pissed on by a kid in crotchless undies, did I become unfussed like the other commuters and adopt a blank-eyed stare: protection against the threat of life falling apart at the opening of those carriage doors.

Language was my biggest obstacle. I felt like I was at the dentist and he was asking me if I had a girlfriend, knowing full well that his hands were jammed into my mouth, and that I was gay. There was something wonderful in an organic, wordless exchange, using the stripped-bare language of the body. But only when it worked.

Even body language failed me. In China the numbers one through nine were counted on one hand using a series of signs. Six, for example, was a fist with the pinky and thumb sticking out wide. Ten involved the middle finger crossing the index finger. I had no idea about this before I came to Beijing, thinking that having ten digits would always mean using two hands.

Despite carrying a notebook everywhere and scribbling down words and phrases over dinner, I wasn't learning fast enough. The book filled quickly, but I remembered Stephen's deal and I started calling language schools.

I was going ga-ga. I was learning to talk and read all over again like a toddler. I needed pals and, the worst thing for me, I needed to be patient.

On weekends at one in the afternoon, still in bed, I would rail at myself: *James, get dressed! Stop looking at porno, you freak. Get up, get up! DO SOMETHING! Surely there's something to do in this giant place you travelled halfway across the world for. Go meet some artists, go to the Summer Palace, the Temple of Heaven, the Llama Temple, all those places you haven't been yet. Go eat those seahorses you saw yesterday then write about how weird it was.*

Instead I would roll over and realise I had no bottled water left. The very idea of going out and getting more sent me into a deep cultural coma. I had never experienced this before while overseas. This was different.

I had culture shock.

Mark, a friend in Sydney who had recently travelled to India, wrote to inform me of my condition.

1. You now truly understand and respect the term 'culture shock'. Back in Sydney, you thought the term was reserved for the ignorant and those scared of change and adventure, both of which you thought you were a master of.
2. You feel as isolated as buggery. Tiny little Jimmy in the middle of big fucking China.
3. 1.3 billion people is 1.3 billion people. For every person you see in Australia, China has 65 of them. That's a lot of people.
4. The people become like props in a play. You start to think that these people don't have personalities. These people don't have families. And life stories. They can't. There's too many of them. If they all did, there would just be too much information.
5. Things are so easy and efficient back home. Nothing fucking works in this place.
6. You find yourself magnetised to familiar brands and for

a deniable period of time you truly feel a connection with all things American. Driving past McDonald's, your heart skips a beat, your stomach rumbles. You begin defending the 'Americanisation' of culture in Australia.

7. You spend a disproportionate amount of time indoors (usually in bed), trying to turn off the ceaseless sights and sounds. Your door becomes your friend when you get home and the enemy when it's time to leave. The inch-thick gateway to the eternal shit-fight that is life for these people.

8. You gain massive respect for the humble yet civilised Western toilet. And you feel like a second-rate animal utilising the sub-human squat style that Asia prefers.

I ticked every box. I was riddled with assumptions and prejudices. How annoying was it that everyone used horns, for chrissake? Even when I knew it was mostly to help navigate the intense traffic and to alert pedestrians, I still reacted with frustration and aggression.

It was the same with the toilet paper in the little plastic bins next to the toilets. I still wanted to flush my toilet paper down, even though I understood the sewerage system couldn't handle it. I even got an email after one blocked-toilet incident. 'Living in China is not like living in EU or USA,' it read. *I'm not from the EU or the USA. I'm from Australia.* 'The equipment is designed in the Chinese style, especially the pipe. The pipe is designed only for polluted water, not for waste paper or sanitary towels. Perhaps most Western people are not used to this. This may bring you some problems and we are really sorry.' It took me months to do the right thing in restaurants: wipe, fold and place in bin. In my own home, I figured forking out a few yuan every three months to unblock a toilet was worth not having to take a pile of poop paper to the public bins every day.

Another source of confusion was the many names for money. One yuan was the principal denomination of China's currency, the Renminbi, also written as RMB, and meaning 'people's currency'. My wallet was fat with wads of pale green yuan bills. The yuan was subdivided into coins that also added bulk to my back pocket: ten jiao, each of ten fen (cents).

Most Chinese, however, referred to the yuan by its nickname, kuai. This catchier way stuck.

I craved emblematic Western things like the *International Herald Tribune* and *The Very Best of Elton John* – things I could completely lose myself in. I suddenly wanted never to see a Chinese bathroom, or cross a Chinese street, or find myself in a Chinese workplace again. Ever.

I needed air. I needed privacy and space. I needed a swim. A pool was always one of the first things I sought out in a foreign city, the best place to meditate. Fifty metres, eight lanes, indoors, good water quality; 25°C is my idea of a safe haven.

In the meditative rhythms of Dongdan Indoor Swimming Pool, I realised how much doubt I'd been living with about my decision to come to Beijing and leave behind everything I loved. My slow stroke reminded me of the hours spent ploughing the Sydney University pool, where I formed the idea to come to China. And as I drummed the water in Beijing, doubt began seeping from my back, my arms and shoulders, into my regular freestyle and out of my fingers. What remained was a strong, steely commitment to stay.

CHAPTER 4

WORKING FOR THE MAO

China Radio International occupied military land on the city's western outskirts, a suburb famous only for its cemetery. In Beijing-speak, 'going to Babaoshan' meant going to die.

Stepping out at Babaoshan subway station, two things caught the eye. The first was a white Ferris wheel. This provided its passengers with a view of the second thing: the China Radio International building.

The travelling World Carnival had squatted in a dust bowl in Babaoshan for several months (the carnival people had chopped down the trees the previous year). While posters showed kids being hurled around rollercoasters, most of the activity was confined to janitors cleaning polyester teddies that would never be won. The rides looked dangerous.

The CRI building was, against this backdrop, a more impressive affair: a fifteen-storey white building with satellite dishes attached to the roof. A darker vertical column cut up through the centre. Its spike reached for the sky. Big gold Chinese characters announced China Radio International down one side, and 'CRI' was written across the top next to the spire's base. Inside, new equipment worth £1.8 million was provided by Siemens Austria and allowed CRI the dubious boast of the 'largest digital broadcasting system of any radio service in the world'.

On a fine day, the eight-year-old facility looked cutting-edge, somehow leaning into the sky as I approached. The red flags lining the driveway gave the impression that Austrian heads of state were paying a polite visit. On a soupy summer day when I couldn't make out the spire from the pollution, the flags drooped.

At the entrance, a PLA soldier station controlled a mechanical concertinaed traffic gate, the type that was popular for most official buildings in Beijing. The soldiers, in red star caps and well-cut uniforms, looked like high-schoolers. Military drills were conducted within the grounds; running in formation around the building, dropping for twenty.

The first guard checked my pass, and with a jerk of his head indicated I could enter.

The second checkpoint was up the stairs and across the elevated driveway and inside the building. (I spied a dry fountain with fluoro-cellophaned stagelights. Fantastically kitsch.) An old man wordlessly shuffled around the entrance and flapped his hand for me to show my pass again. If I got past the armed PLA soldiers, it was this old guy's job to take me out.

What was this place? Why did they build China's biggest radio station, a place where many foreigners worked, all the way out here? But what baffled me the most at the outset was how interviews with the movers and shakers of the capital could occur when it took an hour to get here. Did they come to us? Or did we go to them? How tight were the deadlines if reporters dashed back and forth between downtown meetings and Babaoshan Island? They must edit fast. Maybe I should be nervous.

At first glance the Chinese radio station resembled the ABC. Crusty bain-maries in the office canteen, geriatric PCs, endless middle management and the daily disappearance of my chair were all friendly reminders of home. If I ever started freaking out about working for the communist propaganda machine, at least I could do so on the familiar bad espresso I'd grown to love at the ABC.

The ABC was into its second year of a happy relationship with

CRI, sharing know-how and advice on broadcast infrastructure around Asia, as well as human resources. But that's where the similarities stopped.

Chinese state-run media was worlds away from the cuddlier concept of 'public broadcasting' in Australia. On my first day an intern quizzed me about the ABC.

'The Australian government gives the ABC money to run the corporation,' I explained, 'but it has no say in *how*, really. It's independent.'

'That's stupid,' the intern interrupted.

'Huh?' I stalled.

'Stupid,' she went on. 'Why would the government give money to something that will only criticise them?'

'Yes,' I nodded. 'That *is* a good question.' I fumbled my way through the distinction between public funding and government control, trying not to use the word 'democracy', like playing the boardgame Taboo. 'It's owned by the people,' I concluded.

'So is CRI,' she pointed out. 'The government is ours and so is the station. The People's Republic owns the land, the building, the radio equipment.' Fair point. This was as far as we got on day one: I just didn't know enough about CRI.

Commercial activity was forbidden at the ABC. But at CRI there was no sense that money, politics and journalism were enemies. The station received mixed funding from a number of advertisers (airlines, language schools), and therefore, like other businesses, had commercial interests.

Corporate gifts were great and I was on the take. Having never before worked at a commercial station, this was my first opportunity for perks. Our names were ticked off on rosters for phone cards and branded bath towels (both thoughtful presents for an expat). A bizarre deal with a government importer resulted in the reek of rotting navel oranges, as crates of mouldy fruit grew wet and green under desks. We ignored the stench and the clouds of fruit flies until some weeks later, when the cleaners were allowed into the office (normally off-limits) to dispose of the mess and mop up the slick.

The fact that contra was distributed differently between foreign and Chinese staff was a point of envy for me, a Beijing bachelor. Chinese staff took home a handsomely packaged laundry and bathroom kit put together by leading suppliers from abroad, complete with enzyme-boosted laundry powder, fabric softener, clothes pegs, anti-dandruff shampoo (Beijing was very dry) and, less useful for me, face whitening cream. I was still washing clothes with liquid hand soap. I wanted that pack.

The oddest present was a ten-litre vat of cooking oil derived from nuts that on last reports was still tucked behind my filing cabinet where it went to die. A couple of months after I'd started at CRI, and without warning, Coca-Cola began appearing under our desks. When low, workers self-medicated with a lukewarm can plucked from the Coke case they were using for a footrest. Caffeinated brilliance was followed by deep afternoon slumps and hiccups. Dark rings developed under the eyes of heavy users.

When supplies dwindled, withdrawal set in office-wide. I was once caught fisting the Coke machine. My arm was wedged for an hour after attempting to reach the final can of Coke that had become lodged behind the glass. I was on my knees, up to my elbow – like birthing a cow. A shuffling crowd gathered around me, more concerned about the trapped Coke than my arm, which had turned a bright shade of Chinese red. While some tried to rip me from the machine, others realised that I had the best chance of reaching the last Coke in Babaoshan.

'Keep pushing, James!' someone spoke up, eyes glued to the shiny can.

Building maintenance was called and the next thirty minutes were spent debating the best plan. My arm turned mauve. Then, as if my grandma were speaking to them live from Australia, someone produced a bar of soap and lathered my arm. DJs and radio producers heaved me out of the machine. The Coke can was still trapped inside.

No 'How's your arm?' No 'Are you OK?' The crowd slouched back to their desks to endure a long afternoon without stimulants.

There were two instances when commercialism affected me and my work more than a simple caffeine habit.

The first time, my desk editor asked me to bury paid-for editorial into a business news story. It was blatant. The inflated figures showed the company flogging its nearest competitor. I said no.

'Well, you must,' the desk editor replied. 'You have to, it's your job.' While branded bath towels allowed me to dry myself with something other than a dirty t-shirt, I wasn't prepared to knowingly drop ads into news without telling the listeners. I told her fine, kept it in the system until she logged off, then deleted it. I watched and waited for something bad to happen, but nobody noticed.

The second time, I was given a special task beyond language polishing: to cover a press conference that marked the start of the International Business Ethics and Eastern Wisdom Conference, run by the just-opened Centre for International Business Ethics. About fifty journalists came to Firstar, a boutique French restaurant, to chink crystal glasses of sparkling wine and sample the organic brie. The public relations company staff were tall, young and strikingly pretty. This was my idea of an afternoon off work. Until I was bribed.

At a table with a view of the courtyard's water feature, I opened the press kit. There was an envelope. I was disappointed. Usually there was a leather gift crafted by some indigenous minority of a Chinese province, or a corny corporate present that flashed and beeped. I was thinking, *I come to this press conference and all I get is this lousy stationery*. But I opened it, and there was Chairman Mao staring back at me in triple vision – 300 kuai (about £25) – a lot of money in Beijing. I blushed and closed the envelope quick smart, thinking I was the only one targeted. Then I looked around and saw Chinese journos fingering their envelopes to calculate today's pocket money. Was this corruption? Was this the International Business Ethics part, or the Eastern Wisdom part?

The only person to ask was Stephen. I discreetly texted him on my mobile.

There's money inside my press conference show bag! Argh!

My phone vibrated a moment later.

Hand it back and see what happens. Record everything.

I formulated a plan.

Everyone milled around, tucking into bite-sized crème brûleé. Then it was my chance to interview the speakers face to face. I covered the main points of the conference and, with my hands shaking, I placed my show bag on the table and pulled out the red envelope.

I took a breath. 'I find it strange that at a conference about business ethics I should receive an envelope of 100-kuai notes.'

I felt the exhilaration of confrontation. The two speakers, vice-director of the centre, Stephan Rothlin, and Renmin University celeb-academic Yang Hengda, stared at the microphone. I went in for the tabloid clincher: 'Are you trying to bribe me?'

Tape rolling. I am a Journalist, I am a Journalist: capital J.

A long pause. Rothlin coughed and then laughed to defuse the situation. 'I can assure you we are not bribing you,' he said.

'It's Chinese tradition,' Yang offered, 'to pay for the journalists' taxis, for expenses that journalists, who do a wonderful job, might incur during the course of their work, and as thanks for taking time out of their busy days. If Chinese organisations paid as well as organisations in the West, the tradition might be rethought.'

'But 300 kuai,' I countered, 'we know that you can get across the city for 30 kuai. I'd be fired if I took this back home. As a contribution to the global understanding of business ethics, I'd like to hand back the money.'

'Thank you for your grand gesture, James,' Rothlin said tersely, then signalled that the interview was over.

I felt shabby. One of the hot PR girls approached me, visibly shaken and close to tears. 'What went wrong?' she asked in American-accented English. 'Did we cause offence with the envelope? I'm so sorry. We won't do it next time. Will you still come to the follow-up conference next month?'

I'd flown in the face of saving face.

I rang Stephen on the way back to Babaoshan.

'Well, well, well, Mr Reporter. What happened?'

'I recorded everything and they were pissed off. But what a rort. I'm going to run it tomorrow.'

'You're right. It's not on. Journalism isn't something that can be bought and sold like everything else, though here they think journalists are just like another contractor to be paid for their services.'

'But Stephen, you should have seen the cheeses! I ate them, but suddenly when it's in note form . . .' I faltered.

'Well, next time take the cash and see how you feel. It's a chance for you to face the issues, see where you stand.'

Back at the office my colleagues were appalled that I had handed back the cash. It made them look bad for taking money themselves. Still, it made great audio.

I submitted the story for broadcast on the weekly business programme, *BizChina*.

When the programme aired, my work had been chopped in half, my confrontation gone. No explanation was given, and nothing was heard of the story again.

I was not given another press assignment for four weeks, so I remained Babaoshan-bound. From the fourth-floor window, I watched the Ferris wheel spin and spin, carrying no one, until one day the World Carnival packed itself into trucks and fled the city's fringe.

I have found my new home. It's near the Forbidden City and Tiananmen Square in a district called Nanchizi, home to the toothless draughts-playing Beijingers who look like geriatric Maos. It's beautiful – old Chinese, in the heart of Beijing. You can find my home by navigating a series of *hutong* (inner-city alleyways), clogged with vendors and bicycles; the further in you go, the more tranquil and green it becomes. You pass an old temple and come to double red doors that open onto a communal courtyard linking four terraced apartments made of grey brick. The courtyards are meeting points for neighbours in summer; in winter, they are blanketed white.

A canary whistles in its bamboo cage. There is the distant sound of sawing and hammering. I hope the incessant mandolin from the temple will be as romantic in a few months' time. My light, small, elegant apartment is decked out like my grandma's old place would be, if my grandma were Chinese. Around the corner is a market, packed with sacks of grains and spices, animals and beer.

My landlord is the local auto-mechanic. His shop is always busy, and soon locals know who I am. We forged the deal by email through his English-speaking son, who is my age and studying in Canada.

I move in on a bright Saturday after two weeks of muck and haze. My landlord helps position a desk in the bedroom then stands in the corner, drawing deeply on a cigarette. He watches me. When my laptop appears, he indicates he wants to look.

We are side by side. I cycle through photos of Australia saying what few words I know for home, friends, family and beautiful. I arrive at a sunny photo of my dad and he puts a large, mechanic's hand on my back to stop me.

'*Ni baba*,' he says. We stare at the photo and when I look up I see tears in his eyes. 'Your father,' he murmurs in English.

A moment later he chuckles. He rubs my back then exits through the red doors, leaving a cloud of smoke in the courtyard.

His son emails me that night. 'If there is anything you need, please let my father know. He will do it. You are his guest and you are very welcome.'

Riding the crowded subway to work allowed plenty of time to develop a Chinese pop addiction. I downloaded all the latest hits and pumped up the volume to pass the hour-long commute.

In the summer of 2005, the hottest event was China's version of the global *Idol* craze, which attracted a top-notch sponsor in the form of a dairy company. The TV show was called, in translation, the *Mongolian Cow Yoghurt Super Voice Girl Contest*. At the end of its four-month run, 400 million people tuned in to *Super Girl* for the results of the only universal suffrage allowed in the country: the election of a pop star by telephone and SMS.

People watched the results with democratic zeal; some campaigned in the streets. It was the biggest domestic TV audience in the history of television, roughly the same as if every man, woman and child in the UK, USA and Canada sat in their living rooms and all switched on their sets. (In comparison, 12 million watched the 2005 final of *Pop Idol* in the UK.) China's TV market was enormous, according to numbers in the *Guardian*: 3,000 channels with 40 million new television sets sold a year, and most of the 361 million households in China owning at least one TV.

The winner, Li Yuchun, a 21-year-old tomboy, got millions of votes and thus, the Western press was ecstatic to point out, became the only person in China to have been popularly elected. China's state-run English newspaper, the *China Daily*, smirked, 'How come an imitation of a democratic system ends up selecting the singer who has the least ability to carry a tune?' True, she couldn't sing and she wasn't beautiful. But she was independent, she was assertive, she sang songs written for male singers, and she sang them like men. It was for these reasons – a backlash against traditional femininity by young women – that Li Yuchun became outrageously popular.

But Beijing trends moved quickly, and *Super Girl* faded fast. Soon every Hello Kitty bag-wearer switched his or her ringtone from Li Yuchun to 'Xi Shua Shua!' a song by mainland band, The Flowers.

The fact that 'Xi Shua Shua!' plagiarised a 2003 tune made popular by Japanese duo Puffy AmiYumi was no obstacle to success in China. It sold 200,000 copies in forty days. DJs at Beijing's much-hyped dance clubs hinted at dropping the track for hours with chorus samples. When the song finally played, partiers clambered onto the dance floor. Even cabbies tapped steering wheels in time with the infectious hand-clapping from the four tiny lads with big hair and quirky clothes. I played a game on the subway. I hummed a bar at just-audible levels, then imagined the song spreading like a disease throughout the city as commuters passed it on to whomever they met.

Like all great pop, it was about nothing. It did, however, carry a message strangely in line with several hygiene crackdowns in the run-up to the Olympics. 'Xi Shua Shua!' meant 'Wash, scrub, scrub!'

And it was no coincidence that a song about washing and scrubbing was the soundtrack to my first job, wiping radio scripts clean of imperfections in grammar and spelling for the website or broadcast. The first weeks presented a bewildering range of stories to polish, translated from the original Xinhua news agency wire.

A typical story in the polishing queue, pre-wash-and-dry, would read something like this:

> Central Committee General Office and State Council General Office recently issued 'Opinions on further strengthening and improving the construction and management of minor extracurricular activities'.
>
> It pointed out that the investment by all levels of government dedicated to build the public services, such as young minor's palace, the children's palace, young student activity centre, child activity centre. We must always give priority to social effect and make the effective implementation of the principle of public welfare.

My first cleaning task was to understand the big terms. 'Minor extracurricular activities'? And what are these 'palaces' where minors hang out?

The second wash cycle was to find the reporter responsible for the translation and work out how to make it better. This was tougher than it sounded. Colleagues preferred to shrink from criticism rather than discuss stories on the floor for all to hear. Once located, a whispered discussion followed.

> Me: What are extracurricular activities? I don't understand.
> Reporter: Do you know museums?
> Me: I love museums.
> Reporter: That's extracurricular. Playing sport. Going to activity centres.
> Me: As opposed to going to school?
> Reporter: The things you do when you are not studying.
> Me: So what's wrong with the museums now? Are museums bad here in China? Do kids not get out enough?
> Reporter: Oh no, China has some of the best museums in the world, especially in Beijing.
> Me: Then why do we need to make them better?
> Reporter: It doesn't say.
> Me: It doesn't say?
> Reporter: It doesn't say. [Reporter points to the original fax roll from Xinhua.]
> Me: Oh.

There were dozens of this type of story each day: sleep deprivation among stressed teens, fighting crime in provincial China, housing regulations, a new railway corridor through China's rust belt, new crackdowns and new guidelines of a judicial, cultural and financial nature. Not to mention the endless panda stories. Public service announcements, that's what they were, brought to you by the Standing Committee du Jour under the State Administration of You-Name-It.

I was thrilled when more straightforward propaganda rolled into the queue; the sheer naughtiness of cleaning up communiqués from Central Government. Subtlety, I once thought, could be useful for the modern propagandist. I was wrong. These stories hit me like a speeding Beijing taxi. My favourite was the 'Bilateral Relationships Are Getting Better and Better Every Day' story.

The following steps give some idea of the rules I followed for 'cleaning up' a story.

Step 1. Start with a vague pledge. Use the words 'economy' and 'cooperation'.

The Czech Republic and China pledged on Tuesday to further develop their cooperation in various areas, especially in economy and trade.

Step 2. Mention a multinational juggernaut with lots of exciting foreign names and a slew of documents to be ratified, but make sure both sides don't say anything.

The Czech Republic said it 'wanted to further promote its cooperation with China at different levels and in all fields', while China wanted to 'work together with the Czech Republic to bring their bilateral ties to a higher level'.

Step 3. At least one document needs to be signed – it doesn't matter what, just don't detail the content.

China and the Czech Republic signed the nine-point joint declaration on December 8, 2005 in Prague, making the commitment to promote friendly relations.

Step 4. Lastly, ensure you have something to do tomorrow: mention the next bits of the multi-nation tour.

Hui left Beijing last Wednesday for a four-nation tour, which has already taken him to Poland and the Czech Republic. He is now in Albania.

This was the template, however there was always a chance to add reminders around one of the government's central policy themes. When Vice Premier Hui Liangyu ended up in Albania at the end of his handshaking tour, extra icing was added to the diplomatic cake. *[Albanian Prime Minister Sali] Berisha highlighted that Albania will unswervingly stick to the One-China policy for which Hui expressed his thanks and appreciation.*

Any country, anywhere in the world, and the story was the same. The task was to convey a China orchestrating economic willingness for new world dominance.

Semantics were important and I often slipped up. I called the Taiwan people 'Taiwanese' – the standard treatment in Australia, but one which suggested that Taiwan was a separate nation. I referred to mainland China, rather than the Chinese mainland. I added 'hard-line' to an article about the new Iranian president.

Watching my fumbles from afar, someone in the office sent me an anonymous email.

> Dear James,
>
> Welcome to CRI! It's good to have you on board. I suggest at this moment you can just focus on grammar rather than journalistic standards. I know it is not easy for you as a Western professional, but this organisation is very sensitive about the political aspect of the stuff. We do not criticise foreign governments, that is their business. Be careful.
>
> A lot of news items are purely propaganda and you are not supposed to criticise that much as you did back home if you plan to work for CRI in the long run. Now, just focus on language, rather than the content itself.
>
> Good luck!

After that I decided to keep my head down but I remained shocked and angry that so many people were being duped so often, and seemingly without a second thought. I thought there would be touches of endearingly transparent propaganda around the edges of harder newsmaking. But this was a different kind of journalism.

At university I was taught that journalism was critical to democracy: the 'fourth estate', a vigilant place of great idealism handed down from that mother, the BBC, and from the Vietnam War correspondents.

In China, I was learning that journalism was also critical to monopolistic socialism. It was time to rethink the 'mass' in mass media.

CHAPTER 5

THE CAPTAIN

Foreigners gave the boss of CRI's English service a nickname. We called her Captain Rorschach. She was a daunting psychological test. The Captain stood at no more than 5ft 1in centimetres with piano teacher posture. An unblemished 60-year-old, she sported a severe bob that wouldn't budge in a gale. She smiled with only the bottom half of her face; her eyes remote at all times. The Captain wore crepe-soled shoes. She would creep up on me, suddenly appearing beside me in a lift. She was there too, watching behind the studio glass as I prepared to take an afternoon nap.

It was rumoured that the Captain smoked out dissidents from post-Tiananmen CRI to get a leg-up in the organisation, though it was difficult to know how much of this to put down to expat embellishment. Jenny, a Scottish presenter, told me Rorschach trotted out her impish husband for official events only, and kept her under-achieving son locked in the basement.

Captain Rorschach had a favourite word each month, picked up at some management class on one of her many trips abroad. Her latest was 'frank'. 'I want to be *frank* with you,' she would say. Of course, everyone was terrified when she was frank. It meant things were going to end badly for you that day. Like the day I asked for a week's leave over Christmas.

The timing could not have been worse. Another Australian on exchange from the ABC was mysteriously fired the day before on trumped-up charges, including that she was 'not physically fit to work at the English service'.

The Captain soon materialised beside me at my desk and said, 'Come with me.' God, it was my turn. She led me to a room and shut the door. She took a breath, then let rip.

'I'm going to be *frank*!' Uh oh. 'We have not brought you to China to pay for your fun times in Beijing. You will work! You Western-ers are so manipulative. You think we Chinese are so stupid!' She clenched both fists and shook them at me, her helmet hair like the lid on a boiling pot.

China's scarier traits raced through my head. If I wasn't deported, they would lock me up. Alexander Downer would speak of China's sovereignty and refuse a prisoner swap.

'Your colleagues don't like you, James,' Rorschach continued. 'They think you're young and lazy.'

I was stunned.

'They don't like your work, you know. They have told me so. They think it's simple and not very good,' Rorschach went on at a quieter, more menacing volume. 'Especially that story about the red envelopes.' Our eyes met. 'Such a stupid, *stupid* story.'

Now, this made me angry and I snapped out of my stupor. 'My family is travelling countless miles to see me,' I choked.

'Not my problem!' Rorschach yelled back.

'My contract has Christmas leave entitlement.'

'You won't have a contract soon!' she cried.

Silence held the room. I began mentally preparing my welcome home party.

Rorschach paced along one wall before settling herself into an upholstered chair in the corner. She smoothed down her pantsuit and picked at a loose thread on the arm of the chair.

'They say I'm very lenient, you know,' she decided finally. 'They tell me that. You're very lucky indeed. I will not fire you.' She breathed out. 'Even after everything with that other Australian yesterday.'

She slipped silently from her chair and glided towards the door.

'But you will remain on probation, and you will work the night shift until I say. I am very fair.'

'Yes, madam,' I murmured.

'I hope we can be *frank* again in the future.' She smiled with the bottom of her face and left the room.

CRI started around the time Rorschach was born. As an underground communist station, it broadcast from a cave in the foothills of the Taihang Mountains in north China's Hebei province. XNCR, as it was known then, kept the civil war-torn countryside updated on the liberation. On day one, the Chinese broadcast was accompanied by a Japanese service shooting propaganda across enemy lines, and CRI legend says the first announcer, Japanese Hara Kiyoko, rode to the studio on a donkey and used a torch both to find the microphone and to scare away wolves.

The new capital welcomed XNCR in 1949. The next year the station changed its name to Radio Peking and set up an editorial office within the Central People's Broadcast Station. In the 1960s its only relay station was in communist Albania – the sole Eastern European nation to side with the PRC in the Sino-Soviet split earlier that decade, and one of the first countries to make diplomatic ties with the People's Republic. In 1983 the station changed its name to Radio Beijing, and a decade later to China Radio International to avoid confusion with the capital's own metropolitan radio station.

CRI was now one of the three big branches of state-run broadcast media, next to China National Radio and the alarmingly titled CCTV, all under the control of the State Administration of Radio, Film and Television. The bigwigs in CRI were either directly appointed or approved by the State Administration.

'We often describe ourselves as one of the three biggest international broadcasters in the world after BBC and Voice of America.

So I guess that makes us the biggest in Asia,' one of the CRI channel controllers told me.

CRI offers 1,100 hours of radio programming a day in thirty-eight foreign languages aside from Mandarin and Cantonese, Hakka, Xiamen and Chaozhou dialects. (The year 2004 marked the fortieth anniversary of CRI's coverage of world events in Esperanto.) CRI was heard across the nation on FM frequencies and all around the globe on a combination of short-wave frequencies.

In January 2006, a new CRI service, 91.9 FM, was launched exclusively for Nairobi, Kenya, broadcast in Chinese, English and Swahili. This new station came as the trade relationship between China and the African continent soared to £30 billion a year – China had ninety-eight Chinese-run enterprises on the continent. China was Africa's new economic coloniser. One reason was China's thirst for oil, and two-way deals with oil-rich Nigeria alone were in the billions. Sudan sent 80% of its oil to China, making it China's third-biggest supplier. While America divested from Sudan in 1997 for humanitarian reasons, China continued to invest in the war-torn nation, policing its oil pipelines and voting down peacekeepers with its veto power in the UN. It was the biggest foreign investor in Sudan, a relationship worth £1.7 billion. In 2003, Human Rights Watch accused China of supplying arms to the Arab militias in Darfur.

China's role in Africa was not lost on Kenya's Minister for Information and Communications, Mutahi Kagwe. 'I appreciate the vital role that China has played and continues to play in the economic development of Kenya,' he told China's Xinhua news agency. 'I am convinced that the launch of CRI in Nairobi will open up new possibilities of exchanges as well as creating synergy in our different fields of our social endeavours like culture, tourism and the media.'

Where oil was to be found or Chinese dominance needed to be asserted via the One-China policy, CRI was there to provide lifestyle features, news-you-could-use and upbeat reflections on China's rise. Lhasa, the capital of Tibet, could listen to CRI while most of China's northwest could not.

Drill a hole, sink a mine, put up a receiver. China knew the mass media wasn't simple window-dressing to the clunk and grind of deal making. China did Pomp Politics, and CRI provided well-produced Pomp in all the languages of the world, making Babaoshan the most powerful suburban backwater in China.

In 2006, Liu Yunshan, head of the Chinese Propaganda Department, addressed a mass rally to celebrate CRI's sixty-fifth birthday. CRI was all about the Communist Party, he said. His speech, one long declarative sentence, was carried by Xinhua, and polished by me to make a bit more sense:

> Over the past 65 years, under the correct leadership of the Central Committee, CRI has persisted in taking Marxism-Leninism, Mao Zedong Thought, Deng Xiaoping Theory, the 'scientific development' concept and, in close conjunction with the central work of the party and state and in line with the demands of China's overall diplomatic strategy, introduced China to the world, introduced the world to China, reported the world to the world, vigorously created an international media environment favourable to China, and comprehensively fostered China's good image internationally, thus making an important contribution to the reform, opening up, and modernisation drive, the great cause of China's reunification, the safeguarding of world peace, and the promotion of common development.

It is the fact that CRI broadcasts in the world's two most popular languages, English and Chinese, that gives it so much weight, something made even clearer with the 2008 Olympic Games.

'In twenty years' time,' said then Chancellor of the Exchequer, Gordon Brown during a 2005 speech in Beijing, 'the number of English speakers in China is likely to exceed the number of speakers of English as a first language in the rest of the world.' Valued upwards of £30 billion, in 2005 China was already the world's largest market for English-language services, according to *The Economist*. And it wasn't just the Chinese getting friendly with the lingua franca of globalisation. It worked the other way too – Westerners wanted a piece of the pie, though they didn't always get it right.

One of Coca-Cola's first names in Chinese characters could be transliterated as 'bite the wax tadpole'; KFC's successful 'finger licking good' campaign translated as 'so good, you'll bite your fingers off'. Pepsi had hoped to 'bring more life' to consumers after a can of its refreshing soda. Instead it promised to 'raise your ancestors from the dead'. Today multimillion-dollar branding consultants can dream up the perfect combination of Chinese characters to connote every nuance of a Western brand hitting Chinese shelves.

Being on this sometimes-shaky bridge between languages appealed to me a lot. It was a place where meaning could be contested, where things that could not be translated still had to find currency in English. 'What better way to get to know the culture and language of a new country?' I thought.

One look around Beijing and the need for professional English services was evident. I had my own favourites. One was a CRI radio ad encouraging listeners to write in with their experiences of love to win a bunch of red roses. The on-air promo ended with a male voice, one of the very conservative senior managers, confessing, 'Love is the feeling of being really penetrated.'

But for pure shock value, a directory sign in the Gynaecology and Obstetrics Department of a big Beijing hospital took the gold medal. Reading the list you were directed to the following rooms:

> Emergency Room
> Observation Room
> Obstetrics Centre
> Cunt Examination

I had my work cut out for me.

CHAPTER 6

SWIMMING FOR THE PEOPLE

The Dongdan Indoor Swimming Pool was a boxy sports complex on Chang'an Avenue, the central boulevard around which the rest of the city swung. It was my sanctuary.

The building resembled a high-school facility, immaculate and featureless but for wide windows. Inside, all sense of schoolyard order gave way to an exotic playground for businessmen and sleek fitness freaks. Potted plants stuffed the men's change room. Orchids hung from the ceiling; thorny roses and cacti lined the windowsills. The smell of fertiliser battled with chlorine. The attendants were also hobby botanists, grooming and maintaining the plants between handing out towels.

The first day I went, one swimmer still wet from the pool was standing naked at the windows, cigarette hanging from his mouth, trimming one of the larger variegated grasses with a pair of scissors.

In the shower room, under a maze of rusted piping, a gang of twenty-somethings managed to smoke and wash at the same time, and a skinny man enjoyed a long piss against the concrete wall. I walked on the edges of my feet, as if on hot sand.

The pool itself was Olympic-sized, but everything else resembled a cruise ship. Fluoro deckchairs were occupied by greased-up men in tiny trunks smoking luxuriantly. Pool attendants with perfect hair sat shirtless atop lifeguard towers, flexing their muscles at each other. Bigger plants were suspended from the ceiling and jostled for space with upside-down multicoloured umbrellas that spun independently like colour wheels. Along the walls ran red fairy lights. If I tired of swimming, I could join an enthusiastic game of backgammon or mahjong or spin in the kiddy pool. It was as if we had all been adrift on the Pacific for months.

Each lane was provided with a spit bin at each end. When the plastic bags in the spit bins reached capacity, pool attendants lifted them out with care and emptied the murky contents into the shower stalls.

I took advantage of the unsexy surroundings (there were no moody fellas with perving rituals, or rubbernecking studs like back home) and, for the first time in my life, kicked off my trunks and showered naked at a public pool. I created a stir. My fellow swimmers were curious to see if the rumours about cross-cultural size difference were true. The gang of twenty-somethings, still showering and smoking, scrutinised me. A few older men chortled. One farted. I tried not to freak out and pull my Speedos back on; I'd be a complete loser.

They looked me over then glanced down at each other, trying to judge who of them was the same size as me or bigger. A candidate was elected and there was a protracted effort made for me to collude with him about our dick size. Comparing cocks with six Chinese lads was not the peaceful shower I'd had in mind, but covering up was giving in. So I let it all hang out.

I was learning that masculinity was different in China. As I watched the boys tussle, rumble and hold hands in the gender exclusivity of the change room I felt relief. Whatever my dick size, I was as skinny as these guys and took as much time with my hair.

I finished up, not displeased by our tentative cultural exchange but too embarrassed to join in, and gave a parched palm a little drink of water.

The Annual CRI Swimming Competition was a serious business, designed to encourage workers to exercise and enhance performance for the benefit of productivity. All departments of the station participated. Senior staffer Cui Hong curated the English-service team and was hell-bent on beating the combined South-East Asian services this summer.

'Why don't you come to the training sessions on Tuesdays and Thursdays and you can swim some laps for me?' she said, poised to tick my name off on a red clipboard. She was in her late 40s, in stunning athletic shape, wearing tight gym pants and a hoodie. *Anything to get out of work*, I thought, and signed up.

The pool was in Yuquanlu, a neighbouring suburb to Babaoshan, in the middle of a cluster of houses saluted at all times by a building-sized statue of Mao.

'Have you been to this pool before?' asked Alan. He was Cui Hong's star recruit, a fit, American-born Chinese. 'The first time I came here I truly freaked out,' he shuddered.

Alan was right. The pool was no Dongdan Indoor Swimming Pool with its off-hand botanists. The floors were slimy and the changing rooms rank. Alan changed, carefully balanced on a bench.

For me, training was another opportunity to swim, but also to splash around and talk about work and toilets, both of which were an obsession at the time.

'Listen, you guys think you've got it bad,' Scottish Jenny spluttered after a lap of her famous breaststroke. Jenny was my desk buddy and made CRI life bearable because she talked and no one else did. Together we indulged in sugar, caffeine and cigarettes to surmount the afternoon boredom. She was quickly becoming a best friend.

'Think about it for a moment,' she said. 'Every day, some girl, or even a number of girls in the English service has her period, OK? There's blood everywhere, on the toilet seats, in places you can't imagine.' She dived back in for another lap leaving Alan and me mute. I never again complained about toilets.

After several weeks of intense training, the morning of the competition finally arrived. Red banners festooned the pool. Marshals were appointed from the pool attendants, and a table of officials monitored the scoring and shouted into an overloaded PA system. There was even a camera crew making a documentary. I joined the sizeable throng of English-service supporters and athletes poolside.

Cui Hong had arrived early, clipboard in hand and roster committed to memory, flustered about the late scratching. During the training weeks, Scottish Jenny had had a drunken row with her bike in a car park. Overbalanced and ripened by wine, she fell off the bike and her friend Yoni crashed on top of her. Following the hallowed customs of her highland forefathers, it was only after a few more brews and a sleep that Jenny discovered her fractured shoulder. A smiley CRI correspondent was subbed in at the last minute, and a DJ from EasyFM was also there to lend a few legs of a very free style of freestyle.

I triumphed by half a length in the backstroke, and Alan and I finished one-two in the men's freestyle. Together, Alan and I romped it home in the men's relay by a length.

The final event was the novelty race in which we had to race the lightest member of our team atop a blow-up mattress for fifty metres. We threw our tiny workmate Ya Jie onto the inflatable. Me and another guy would take the sides of the craft with Alan kicking out back. In lane four, the South-East Asians watched our practice effort and quickly rearranged themselves at the front of the craft.

The starter's gun cracked and our limbs pumped. I became tangled in the lane rope, sending the craft careering starboard. Ya Jie shouted directions. The crowd went wild. I regained my grip and we corrected, but it was too late. The South-East Asians had completed the most competent and humourless novelty race in the history of novelty races, and watched us blunder into the blocks exhausted. Ya Jie broke down in sobs of laughter. We'd come last.

The teams gathered around the scorers' desk for the final results.

I was on a high – I usually hate team sports, but felt a real connection with these guys now. After much deliberation the top three were announced. The news took a while to filter out through the various languages of the station, but we soon learned that the English service was narrowly beaten. But not by the South-East Asians. By the news room from level four. Cui Hong insisted that while they had consistent performers in the older age groups, they were nowhere near as fast as us.

The next day, under my desk, was a large plastic yellow box on wheels, a present for my participation.

'Jimmy boy, what is it?' my spiky-haired colleague Wang Xiaoke asked.

'It's a South Korean clothes steamer!' I gasped. Wang Xiaoke cleaned her glasses on her overalls and together we checked out the box. The instructions were complete with overjoyed South Koreans displaying how the steamer could also be used to unkink curtains and curl your hair. There were also two white bathing caps with Chinese flags on their sides. I felt like I was on the training team for the 2008 Olympic Games.

That afternoon I sat on the yellow box in the middle of the subway carriage and napped drowsily in the heat. I felt like a champion.

WANG LU

In 2005, Wang Lu was chosen to give CRI an identity makeover. It was an apt job for the 34-year-old host of the cult-hit radio programme *Joy FM*, who also went by the English name Jade. She transformed herself daily. Sporty Jade arrived at the studio in a tight velour tracksuit, hair up, gym bag swinging. Power Jade had a decisive walk in an open-necked man's shirt and Wall Street suit, her strong jawline emphasised by blush. Posh Jade wore frills, her eyes made up big with glitter and lips dolled red. Slutty Jade knew just the right length skirt to wear.

When CRI was handed a new FM frequency by the State Administration of Radio, Film and Television, Wang Lu had an idea to go station-wide with a bilingual broadcast of music and talk for the growing number of Chinese living and working in English. A true radio revolution, it would be a first in mainland China.

Wang Lu was appointed channel controller of CRI's reworked EasyFM 91.5. Over six months she ramped up her staff to thirty, including new recruits like me. Wang Lu poached me from the polishing room to prepare interview features: how to save water in your home, how to sit stress-free exams, how to pamper your dog in the year of the dog. I also presented the daily business report. It was live, too, which was still rare at control-freaky CRI.

Wang Lu was a textbook high-achiever. CRI was too small to contain her. In her 20s she held down four jobs, including her CRI evening radio show. She had been the host of *Fashion Circles*, a high-fashion show aired on Beijing Television. On CCTV's English station, she hosted *Centre Stage*, a nightly presentation of traditional Chinese performing arts. And she had been headhunted by Sony's joint venture in China, Shanghai Epic, for her street-cred. As international marketing manager she selected international titles to be released in China, handled the paperwork, made marketing plans and executed them.

For eleven years, Wang Lu had no time for friends or hobbies. Work was king, and she loved the money. She perfected her English at CRI and was awarded a government scholarship to study for one year at the University of Westminster in London.

Were her colleagues jealous of her success? 'Oh yeah,' she says. 'I wanted to save trouble by quitting but the boss wouldn't let me. Now I thank him for that, and I think whoever is benefiting from what I'm doing now should thank him for that, too. It's just a matter of time before I can show my colleagues that he made the right decision.'

We had met for an unprecedented and candid discussion after I'd left CRI. I found myself disarmed by her confidence, by her honesty. It went against everything I knew about Chinese managers, especially those that ran state-run organisations.

'Once labelled, do the labels stick?' I ask her.

'Yes. Yes,' she agrees. 'There was a lot of hesitation over whether they really wanted to appoint me as the channel controller. There was a very big debate at the very top level, and in the end it was the big boss who said "give it a try, it's my call".'

Regardless of whether the managers liked the vision of Wang Lu's bilingual station or not, they loathed Wang Lu. Nine out of the ten panellists voted against her appointment but voting didn't matter in the end. Again, and for what reason Wang Lu doesn't know, the boss looked upon her kindly.

'I want to change our status at CRI from being in the minority to being part of the mainstream,' she says, 'because I do see that potential. I want this channel to cater to the "internationalised" Chinese. They are China's hope in the future, the driving force behind China's urban development. I also think they are the community that Western countries want to have access to.'

EasyFM's listeners are young, upwardly mobile and cash-rich. Their average age is 28. They are uniformly white-collar, part of China's booming middle class: engineers, managers, students, teachers, government workers, designers and media people. They earn a good middle-class salary of 6,000 kuai per month (around £400), which is what a Chinese CRI employee earns. This then enables the middle-class kit of an apartment in Beijing's west, a kick-ass mobile phone, TVs and a nice sofa. Over 40% of EasyFM's listeners now own cars. Around 80% have credit cards, and most have two.

'If we can service them well,' says Wang Lu, 'we have done an excellent job. That's my biggest ambition.' Online discussion forums on EasyFM's website target the middle-class attitudes of their listeners, and deal with buzz topics of the day. Listeners weigh in on questions such as 'The higher your education, the better?' and 'What would you consider a rip-off?' The forums also host discussions on two of the three 'Ts': Tibet and Taiwan, but not yet Tiananmen. The forums are moderated and the issues controlled. But gone are the days of sweeping these issues entirely under the carpet.

Podcasts, high-quality internet streaming, TV set-top boxes and mobile phones are all changing the way that CRI listeners enjoy their station. Still, most listeners remain in the big cities where CRI has FM frequencies and can launch billboard and bus advertising campaigns: Beijing, Shanghai, Lanzhou, Xiamen, Hefei and Lhasa.

'When you grasp a second language, your entire life experience – your world, the size of your world – doubles,' says Wang Lu. 'It does get you closer to the truth. It does remind you to think twice.' Now English-speaking Chinese can think twice using one domestic channel.

Interestingly, the decision to go bilingual was backed up by zero market research. 'The general sense that we must grow, that we must expand, is a much more important reason than the logic behind what we should do on which platform,' she explains. 'So when the opportunity presented itself to launch another channel we concluded that we wanted a channel first and then looked for the reasons why and how to reposition. It's really a matter of looking at new opportunities and then reshaping our business strategy.'

Market research, observes Wang Lu, 'happens in an ideal world'. Marx would have purred. 'In China as an emerging market, the people who have control of the resources will have the luxury to experiment with it. Because everything is run by the government, whether a new channel will prosper or not is just a secondary thought.'

Advertising is a tiny 4% of CRI's revenue, so there's no commercial imperative to conduct market research. They prosper on just less than one billion kuai per year (around £80 million) from government allocations. While advertising does represent a move to becoming more competitive, losing the 4% is a price the organisation can well afford.

At Sony, Wang Lu worked with Americans every day and was dismayed watching them jump hurdles put there by the Chinese government. Yet she has encountered pressures in the world of state-run media, too.

Beijing's dog population was one example. According to the Beijing Public Security Bureau, this population had grown fivefold since 1994 to over half a million pooches. In a bid to stop the spread of rabies in the capital from unregistered dogs, the government began a culling programme: they called it 'Civilising Dog Keeping'. Culling meant clubbing. Dogs taller than 35 centimetres were indiscriminately impounded, Hong Kong's *South China Morning Post* reported. New laws limited each family to one pet dog, and were instantly dubbed by the Western press as China's new 'One Dog Policy'.

Beijingers love their dogs; they dress them in knitted cardigans for winter, and even wipe their bums. Wang Lu was told not to cover the story. 'I received advice not to take an opinion on the radio either way,' she said. 'As a dog lover, it was hard.'

No official number of dogs killed was given, though *South China Morning Post* claimed it was 'tens of thousands'. So damning was the flak from the foreign press and Beijingers that Hu Jintao, the president, reportedly ordered an end to the culling himself.

'Sometimes I think the government's intentions are good,' says Wang Lu. 'I think deep down they mean well. They just need a lesson in public relations skills.'

'Do you think what is acceptable has changed over your time at CRI?'

'The basic things haven't changed. The heart of the political matters in China hasn't changed, though the Chinese people are opening up their minds. I think we hear more voices now than twenty years ago. So we may not be developing at full speed, but we're moving in the right direction. And besides, we have 5,000 years of history, so you can't expect us to become a different nation overnight. Western media or Western governments are so anxious to change the way we do things, the way we see things, they tend to go to the other extreme. But if you combine the two extremes you might get closer to the truth.'

It's this middle ground between East and West, and old and new that, as an outsider, Wang Lu has had to navigate to be successful at CRI. The fight isn't only with the older generation. If she's viewed as a rebel by the old guard, she struggles to keep pace with the new. 'I feel like a nanny right now! Like a grandma talking to my team members. Because they are something like ten years younger than I am, and you know, now three or four years will make a different generation. So they will have different interests. They will have new values, very different from mine. So I feel like I'm living in those clashes on a daily basis. I feel like the last of the Mohicans!'

With other students from her university Wang Lu was witness to the 1989 student upheaval. She was neither on the side of the students, nor the government, she says. When Wang Lu sat the exam for CRI after completing her university degree, she was asked if she was 'political' – meaning, was she for or against the government.

'I told them I was apolitical,' said Wang Lu. She hasn't made a political mistake yet, she says, because she doesn't play the political game. This is Wang Lu's careful and deliberate balancing act.

She says she still has a lot to contribute if the management continues to want her. And to do it, to continue the reform, she's looking for ambitions that fit with her new-breed, business-smart attitudes.

'I want to clone myself,' she says seriously. 'I need a whole team of Jades.'

CHAPTER 7

NIU BI

'*Nimen shi niu bi!*' hollered one reveller from the depths of the mosh pit. The coveted punk compliment, the ultimate Beijing blessing. 'You guys are cows' cunts!'

Before his large sweaty body slapped once more against the pit's frontline, which was advancing towards the lead singer, I was surprised to read the back of his t-shirt in English. 'Rock music is perhaps the single most shared experience of young people around the globe.'

I blinked, *that was too good to be true*. As the singer flirted with the mosh pit, I hoped with my toes the t-shirt was a prophecy. That we weren't that different, after all.

From the outside, Nameless Highland (*Wuming Gaodi*), resembled a saloon of America's West, tucked incongruously between apartments near the Yi Yuan hospital. The letters 'bar' in red neon and fastened high on a wooden gable called from a distance. A beer mug and musical notes glowed blue and green.

But this place didn't summon hungry cowboys, it raised the Chinese underground. Mohawks and mullets fifteen-deep queued to get in. It cost 20 kuai (£1.60) depending on the band. Inside were Chinese males with piercings and their thugged-out girlfriends. Typically bright Chinese skin was obscured with eye makeup. There were foreigners here of all ages, mainly students from nearby Haidian with their Chinese pals.

Inside, the bar was army-themed. Its logo was a silhouette of a soldier holding a gun, behind the stage was a wall of fatigues, and on the ceiling a coalition of flags that fairly represented the audience: American, French, Chinese, British.

The music, however, was from China's small galaxy of next-generation rock, punk and electronic, bands including Hang on the Box, Salumi, Joyside, New Pants, Lonely China Day.

I've never seen a hungrier crowd more animated. The hint of a danceable beat from ironic New Pants, or a call to mosh was enough to send it lurching. One surge broke the perimeter of the dance floor and sent beer flying over faces to lubricate the singing of grittier songs. I could feel the heat of bodies, like walking into a primary school classroom after summer lunch.

The night was a promotional event showcasing label-mates from Modern Sky Entertainment, China's longest-running and largest alternative music company. Despite the thoroughbred homegrown indie lineup, the bar's sound system was hardwired like its hardwood surrounds to an American palette for icons. Eric Clapton, Whitney Houston, Rick Astley and Lionel Ritchie belted out songs between sets. Western influence could be felt in the Chinese tunes too. The lead singer from Wednesday's Trip was first out with a solo set, her voice and guitar like Joni Mitchell's. Soft love ballads drew a swaying few to the front. Salumi flew in next on laptop and keys. He sounded like a deranged, solo Daft Punk. A bedroom musician but with more clout, he welded happy hardcore with darker material and then pared it back to enlightening moments of quiet. 'It's like Michael Nyman on acid,' Stephen leaned in to say. He was my regular date to Nameless Highland.

There was a small circuit of well-publicised rock bars that drew regular crowds. What? Bar was a crusty brick and timber venue on the west side of the Forbidden City. Super-green guitar bands played here, where they could reach out and touch the audience and the keg of home brew. Yugong Yishan sat across from the Workers' Stadium in Sanlitun in what looked like a demountable classroom. An eclectic mix of rock, jazz, electronica, local and visiting acts played there every night through the best sound system in the city. With much of Sanlitun under the sledgehammer, this place was under the constant threat of being *chai*'ed. (*Chai* was the symbol spraypainted on the side of buildings marking them for demolition.)

The New Get Lucky Bar offered a folksy lineup during the week of Uyghur troubadours from Xinjiang. Big, noisy bands filled the weekend slots. Dos Kolegos was in the grounds of a surreal drive-in cinema complex on Liangmaqiao Lu, past the Kempinski Hotel. Every Tuesday night it hosted Beijing's best experimental music artists. In summer, hundreds came to drink beer and sit on the grass outside to watch rock bands play in the balmy, mosquito-annoyed night.

The Green Beijing Rock Festival at the drive-in (the Beijing Feng-huayuan Car Theatre) was my first dive into Beijing's rock scene and it was held over several weekends in August and September. Blue, red and green fairy lights garlanded the trees along the path north of Chaoyang Park. Several restaurants, one with ducks and rabbits snuffling in a pen, looked onto a central lake that had a cooling, but smelly, effect on the park. Inside further, beyond the gates, the movie posters and the ticketing booth, a cumulonimbus of barbecue smoke rose from the *yang rou chuanr* (lamb skewer) masters holding hairdryers to drive the coals. Twenty rock bands performed over the three Saturday nights here in the main area where the cars would normally be. The festival had a nominal enviro theme, though mounds of dumped garbage spoke otherwise.

A sublime band called Second Hand Rose (*Ershou Meigui*) was among the first to play. I was introduced to Stephen's friend Wang Miao, a 23-year-old drummer from a now-defunct Beijing rock band, who told me he had a poster of Second Hand Rose on his bedroom wall. The lead singer Liang Long routinely appeared in a *qipao*, a traditional Chinese dress, makeup and long hair straightened and woven with roses. His music was glory rock, sexy and funny, combining traditional instruments with rock essentials. Catchy tunes and a camp stage routine made up for my lack of language.

Stephen, in checks and cords and tanned from a recent trekking adventure through Yunnan, shouted '*Niu bi!*' and threw a full cup of beer across the heads of those in the mosh. Meanwhile, Scottish Jenny, her arm in a sling from the bike accident that prevented her from swimming, was attempting to commandeer a milk-van by climbing through its window.

At the festival, I picked up a swag of CDs and began my education in Chinese rock. That's how I first heard Rebuilding the Rights of Statues, Nameless Highland's headline act.

The first time I heard this band on CD, I knew I'd discovered the soundtrack of my Beijing. Their sound was like getting out of a taxi and having your face filled with dust. But underneath the vocal rage and thick punky chords they had a tender underbelly. If there was one band likely to cut it on the international stage, it was these guys.

I first saw them play at Dos Kolegos. The lead singer Hua Dong contorted to the music, at times up on his toes like Michael Jackson, sweeping his arm across his neck and flicking his hand. Liu Min, the tiny bassist, added occasional back-up yelps and morbid squeals like an elf deprived of Christmas. The drummer's beat was unrelenting. They were efficient musicians with racy lyrics: 'Hang the police, hang the police before we're all murdered.' They also sang about a mother mourning the loss of her son in Tiananmen Square.

On stage the threesome faced slightly inwards, like they were singing to each other. I found that both defiant and secretive – just like Beijing.

At Nameless Highland, trembling bass, clanging, shimmering guitars and aggressive vocals gave the band a haunted-house feel. 'The stories that you told on me are not the truth,' bellowed Hua Dong. 'They are not the truth you know? They pushed me into the cage and taught me how to be a monkey!' 25-year-old Liu Min, her hair somehow blacker than other hair – like the girl who sat at the back of the classroom and drew bleeding rabbits in her diary – yipped at the microphone through a heavy fringe.

Not just any band gets the punk tag *niu bi*, so I decided to learn more about them and follow their story.

A brief aside. I never did get a satisfactory explanation for why *niu bi* means 'cool'. Something about cows' vaginas being really big and impressive.

CHAPTER 8

HITTING
THE ROCK CEILING

Liu Min is studying plane tickets. She puts the envelope in her handbag before peering into a suitcase. She has just packed tea leaves into her carry-on bag. She doesn't like American coffee. Hua Dong, her boyfriend, is repacking his clothes. He inspects a brown sleeveless jacket on the couch, approves it, and shoves it into a plastic bag for the plane.

It's snowing in the northeast of America right now. Hua Dong's parents, intellectuals in China's south, told him to pack warm clothes. That's all parents are worried about.

Liu Min double-checks the flight times and the weather online, while Hua Dong busies himself putting his guitar into a new hard case.

The apartment that Liu Min and Hua Dong share seems infected by the mild chaos of the Beijing street. They've just been given their visas today, one day before they fly.

'I'm more prepared than my luggage is,' Hua Dong says with a small, embarrassed laugh. He checks strings for his guitar. Guitar strings are expensive in the States so he is taking his own. They fill most of the case. 'If we have any difficulties or I have to eat McDonald's for a whole month, then I'll definitely miss Beijing!' he giggles. He hunts around in his CD wallet and proudly presents a sticker. 'Gang of Four', it reads. 'This is totally my favourite band,' he says, and peels off the backing. He carefully aligns it to the edges of his travelling guitar case and pats the sticker down. It is a reminder of his musical roots – English post-punk of the late 1970s and early 1980s.

Tomorrow, Rebuilding the Rights of Statues – Re-TROS for short – will be one of the first-ever Chinese bands to tour the United States. They will be the first, along with tour mates Lonely China Day, to license their Chinese-made album to a US label and compete for attention, and sales, in the world's most competitive music market.

'Mentally I'm prepared. There's no problem with playing or rehearsing with the band,' Hua Dong says in an interview, pre-flight. Excitement banks up in his voice and eventually comes out as giggles. 'The three of us have been together for three and a half years now, and we've lived together over this period. We're bound to rub each other up the wrong way sometimes, we're human after all. But we have bigger things to accomplish,' he says in Politburo-style determination, 'and we should set aside our minor differences to focus on the big picture.'

That's the bizarre dare. China rocking America to the sound of the British New Wave. In a global music industry hungry for the next big thing, Rebuilding the Rights of Statues may well be the novelty that carves a niche for Chinese punk music in the West.

Promoters, label managers, film-makers, venture capitalists, commentators and journalists (like me), are all circling in around the idea that anything Chinese, in the run-up to the Olympics, turns water into Western wine. Japanese bands achieved quirky heights in America in the 1990s. China is next.

In Beijing, the alternative music scene is not developing fast enough to accommodate the growing restlessness and desire among musicians for legitimacy. Artists at the top here lust for more.

'It might be that we've reached the ceiling in Beijing,' says 30-year-old Hua Dong. 'Perhaps this is as far as we will get. Even if we keep it up for the next few years. But I'm sure that the top in America is up here,' he indicates a level above his head. 'And it'll take me another ten years to get there. So these next ten years will be very interesting.

'If you can get people to notice you, if you can make a name for yourself, then you can pretty much hold your own anywhere else in the world. To put it another way, America is like a pyramid for some things. If you can get to the top, then coming down and going to other places will be easy.'

Hua Dong adds in precise language, 'Even The Beatles wanted to conquer America.'

It's evident that Rebuilding the Rights of Statues doesn't want to be a Chinese band. It wants to be international. 'The first time I heard post-punk music was from a friend,' says Hua Dong. 'It was twelve years ago. He gave me heaps of CDs, like Echo and the Bunnymen and The Cure. Everything about post-punk along with some books and magazines about post-punk culture.' His bedroom shelves teeter with the records: Joy Division, Bauhaus and more. I never once heard Hua Dong mention a Chinese influence, and all the band's songs are in English.

But cultural borrowing or referencing – standard practice in the pop world – is more complex in China. Bands like The White Stripes or The Strokes draw on decades of music history to shape their sound. Re-TROS' access to a cultural history of pop and rock was delayed by state controls.

Hua Dong's punk education started in the mid-1990s, twenty-plus years after these post-punk bands found Western ears. Rock music for Hua Dong, and most active Beijing musicians, came via washed-up plastic waste from the West.

According to the Japan External Trade Organisation, China remains the world's largest importer of waste. In 2004, China imported over 4.1 million tonnes of recyclable plastic waste, including CDs, mainly from Germany, Belgium and the Netherlands, a trend that has continued from the 1990s.

The formula is this: scissors + plastic = rock. In the 1990s, when

British or US warehouses cleared discontinued CDs, they sold them as scrap and shipped them to China in their hundreds of thousands, bound for recycling in the southern ports. Or so they thought.

Exporters clipped the edge of CDs or sawed out a chunk from the case to indicate they couldn't be resold. As fate would have it, the plastic itself wasn't recycled, the culture contained on the CDs was. Everything imaginable was there but it was the eclectic stuff, anything too foreign, niche or immoral for Chinese distributors to make any profit from that found eager collectors. This alt-trash was a history lesson in the greats: Tom Waits, Iggy Pop, the Sex Pistols, Leonard Cohen, Blur, The Cure, Depeche Mode, Radiohead, Björk, Bob Dylan, Gang of Four.

Dakou was the Chinese word given to these CDs, sold alongside pirated discs in street markets and stores in the know. 'Da' here means to hit. 'Kou' is a cut. *Dakou* could still be played because most CD players scan from the inside of the disc to the outside. Only the last tracks were lost.

Beijing musicians were hungry for new sounds after the cataclysm of the Cultural Revolution. *Dakou* CDs became icons of a movement, writes Jeroen de Kloet, a researcher into contemporary Chinese rock, and an emerging group of musicians and artists went on to call itself the *dakou* generation.

This mini-history of the *dakou* is also a metaphor for how the West exports its culture generally: damaged, sometimes abandoned if not already syndicated. But the cut was not a mark of inferiority for the *dakou* generation; it was a surprise, an opportunity to create something new.

From the beginning, Rebuilding the Rights of Statues had its dreams cut from the same global machine as the *dakou*. It wanted to be of the world, rather than simply of China. But in doing so, it ran the risk, like all Chinese bands, of being regarded as the unworthy remnants of washed-up Western culture. Visitors to Beijing, expecting to hear 'world music' or traditional Chinese instruments fused with the sounds of an industrialised country, are disappointed when they encounter a weekend of Coldplay sound-alikes, often singing in English, and often not very well.

Re-TROS formed in April 2003 in the Sichuan province capital of Chengdu. Liu Min, the bassist, had been in an all-girl punk band, U235. The drummer Ma Hui had his own band in Lanzhou, in the Gansu province. And the lead singer, the soft-spoken, handsome Hua Dong was the drummer in PK14 (a drawcard of the Beijing music scene).

Chengdu didn't cut it, though. And the only way out of China was through Beijing.

Beijing occupied high ground in a country flooded by Hong Kong and Taiwan pop, in buses, restaurants, museums, bathrooms and lifts. KTV, aka karaoke, was the most popular activity for young people, in Beijing too. Whole weekends were spent trawling through dreary pop menus, high on Sprite. KTV was set in mazes of small rooms in dazzling buildings, and it was cheap. I was invited to one session in a KTV megaplex north of the Lama Temple, whose universe contained whole armies of waiters and an etiquette with which I was unacquainted. Luckily, Beijing provided alternative entertainment.

Re-TROS' debut EP *Cut Off!* paved the way for success in their new home. Brian Eno had been in town checking out Modern Sky Records as *Cut Off!* was being mastered and asked to contribute keyboards to a few tracks. One, 'A Death Bed Song', made it to the record. Two national tours followed and the promoters at Modern Sky were surprised by big turnouts. 'When they toured in China,' says Jin, 28, the band's manager, 'all the venues were packed. But the record sales were really low. You'd think they sold 20,000 copies! But really it was just a few thousand.'

More than 5,000 to be exact, after a year and half on the shelves. Jin says that's 'not bad' considering the degree of piracy. 'The biggest problem is still the internet,' Jin says. Popular P2P computer programs like KuGoo (a pun on 'Cool Dog') count more than half a million daily users who share music online.

One other potential problem that Re-TROS has managed to circumvent is that of censorship. Every lyric must be submitted to the Ministry of Culture for approval. Distribution remains controlled, and publishing music requires a government-issued licence. 'They check everything,' says Jin from Modern Sky. So it's more practical to sing in English than Chinese.

The Ministry is on the lookout for anything overtly political, inflammatory or rude; swear words are a no-no. There is a lot of debate in the Modern Sky offices about what will or will not get caught up in the system. 'If it's OK, they give you a number and you pay the money,' Jin explains. 'Then that's it.'

Rebuilding's first album dodged the censors. This is despite *Cut Off!* being threaded – to the native English-speaker's ear – with blatant political allusions. 'Boys in Cage' is a rollicking punk song about blood in Tiananmen Square:

> Boys in cage, I play you fools,
> Cause you knew the truth about that June.
> It was a long long time ago. Boys In Cage.
> Blood at the Square.

In 'If the Monkey Becomes (to be) the King', Hua Dong hoots like a chimp:

> They kill your men, your women,
> Your children, your futures, your minds
> Your bodies and your music.
> This country belongs to the monkey.

The song is an allusion to the ribald Chinese classic of 500 years ago, *Journey to the West*. Sun Wukong, aka 'the Monkey King' is the playful disciple of Buddhist monk Xuan Zang who is on a pilgrimage to India to recover religious texts. Chairman Mao liked to compare himself to the Monkey King, which scholars say is a satire about power gone crazy. For Mao, the story was an allegory for revolution without compromise. In his own speeches, Mao invited comparisons to the Monkey King, holding himself up as a rebel who resisted authority and 'paid no heed to the law or to Heaven'.

The Monkey has become the king, Hua Dong's lyrics suggest, and the country has descended into chaos. But the band denies that the song is explicitly about China. 'It's really not,' Hua Dong says. 'I don't really know what the word "political" specifically means. I just want to tell people what I know, what I see.'

Liu Min is slumped beneath the New York City subway map. She is 10,000 kilometres from home. Her eyes are closed behind prescription glasses in light steel frames. A big knitted sweater softens her look.

At the Brooklyn café earlier, Liu Min stared blankly into her tea while the tour party talked shop and geared up for moving onto the next city of the tour.

The screech of carriage brakes is like a parade of drunken tin-whistlers. The doors open and close. Liu Min is normally taciturn but she hasn't spoken a word today. Not to Hua Dong, not to the tour manager Matthew Kagler from Tag Team records. Not to me, the journalist in tow with a camera and a notepad.

Sitting next to her on the subway seat, Hua Dong looks around, trying to assemble America into a comprehensible whole. His eyes are wide but he is inscrutable. I've seen this look before, on my own face in the mirror at the Friendship Hotel: culture shock.

The band had made $900 the night before at their second New York gig, but Liu Min and Hua Dong had had a fight; one of the guitars was out of tune. I wanted to speak to them after the show, but was persuaded not to get in the middle of something. They have been on the road for a week. Many of the mid-west shows in the States were poorly attended, Chicago especially bombed. Now in New York they haven't had time to get their bearings and in a few hours will be back on the road, driving through the Carolinas to the South By Southwest music showcase in Austin, Texas.

I ask Hua Dong later if things have changed since being in America. 'When we arrived at the airport and got off the plane,' he tells me, 'I was scared because the flight from Chicago to Minneapolis had been cancelled. We didn't know what to do. We didn't have anyone coming to meet us. We were in a totally foreign country and unfamiliar city, so we were a little bit anxious.'

The truth is their experience of being in America has been overwhelming. Before they even played in New York they were wheeled into the ABC studios for an interview on *Mix*, an entertainment news wrap-up. Hua Dong had to conduct the interview in English. Flatscreen plasmas showed the video clip of 'Hang the Police', and labelled them as 'China's number one punk band'. Lights, makeup and that saturated blue of network television.

'Over one billion people have heard the band Re-TROS. Have *you*?' the presenter with the hair said to camera. Predictably, the questions avoided any reference to the music. It was about China. About restrictions. About growing up in a communist country. About misconceptions between the East and the West.

It's the band's first taste of this cruel and inevitable irony. The band's appeal, perhaps its only appeal to a US audience, is that it's *Chinese*.

'I know that a lot of people are coming to see us perform because we're a band from China,' says Hua Dong. 'This makes me nervous, but there's nothing I can do about it. I hope that gradually more people will come see us because we're a band and not just because we're a band from China.'

For now, the band is in a machine milking its Chinese-ness for all it's worth. 'The fact that they're from China helps me a lot,' says Michael LoJudice, the US promoter and entrepreneur kick-starting the New York branch of Modern Sky Entertainment China. 'I mean, you know, would they be on ABC news and NPR and the *New York Times* and everything else without having released a record? No.'

But then he goes onto say that, 'Of any band in China, they're gonna love Re-TROS. They're it. They're it. Totally. They could be a band in New York right now. Their live show is amazing. It's an interesting story, you know. There's a guy-girl thing. Just from an asshole music-industry-guy perspective, all that stuff's there.'

Michael LoJudice says the word 'cool' once every thirty seconds, and cool sounds better in an American accent. LoJudice understands buzz. 'You know: cool. Chinese. Lifestyle. Kids. You know. Whatever.'

LoJudice, 30, is the kind of dude who at 22 was being invited to the New York loft owned by Ben and Claire (Lee and Danes) to party with the Beastie Boys for Ben's 21st birthday. 'I was throwing water balloons out the window on people with guys from Spacehog. And I got into an argument with Janeane Garofalo, cos I was, like, so drunk. Michael Stipe was there.'

He's chatty about the plethora of business opportunities in China. 'Everybody wants to do something in China, but nobody's really reached out to these companies before, and they haven't had a relationship over there to do anything with. Now they do.'

In the world of American music promotion there's no room for Chinese subtlety, and Michael has been in the business for ten years. He's a workaholic. Which is lucky, because this is the biggest shit Michael has ever done. 'It's a first of its kind. We're a Chinese record label,' long pause, '. . . in the US.'

With a nose refined for the next big thing, Michael had sniffed China in the wind for a while. He travelled to Beijing keen to explore the independent music scene. He talked his way into the Modern Sky offices, located inside a boring West Third Ring Road apartment block north of the CCTV tower, and in no time was staying with the founder and boss, Shen Li Hui. Shen, 36, was the frontman for one of Beijing's first pop-rock bands, Sober, whose debut record launched the company in 1997. The two indy music men hit it off and LoJudice stayed for three months. He partied with some of the label's fifteen bands, and drew up financials to launch Modern Sky in the West.

What he saw in Modern Sky sent shivers down his music industry spine. 'I mean for China, a country with one point whatever
billion people, this ever-growing economy, this ever-growing middle class, there's no other company that's really representing *coolness*
from Chinese people.' There are some other expat-driven companies, he says, but they're 'not insiders, and they are not doing it in
a cool way'.

When I spoke to Shen in the Modern Sky offices, he sounded a
typical note of caution, suggesting this move into the States was a
softly-softly affair. 'Americans have their own way of seeing our prod-
ucts and they are pretty business-savvy,' he said. 'There are many
possibilities in America. We have a specific plan about how to make
this work, though I don't know if I will win the gamble or not.'

Michael is not so reserved. Especially when it comes to Rebuilding the Rights of Statues. 'I think they're gonna be big! I think
they're gonna be famous in America.'

The American licensee shares Michael's enthusiasm. 'I would
not have signed Re-TROS had I thought they wouldn't make me
money,' says Tag Team's Matthew Kagler. 'And I think that they
can definitely shift some units.' There's some irony in the way Matthew adopts quotation marks with his fingers in the air when he
says 'shift some units', but not much.

'Look,' says Kagler. 'There's a specific way we *have* to market
it. It's the only way to market it. It has to incorporate the Chinese
whatever into it.'

The band's first New York show was on Manhattan's Lower East
Side in a tiny venue called Cake Shop. Rebuilding played to about
thirty people, a number that swelled for the headliners, Brooklyn
quartet Detachment Kit. I invited two friends, Lisa, a music lover
and audio engineer, and Lauryn, a New York film-maker and source
of obscure B-sides. Both became instant fans.

The second show at the established alternative music stronghold
Southpaw proved more successful. A packed audience, and the
merchandise moved.

But the next day, the band was despondent before its long drive to Texas. Its American journey, like other great American road trips, centres on a prevailing question of identity. Is being Chinese a good enough reason to get people along to shows? And what about the music?

I remember Hua Dong's comment about The Beatles conquering America. America teaches anyone that it's a long way to the top, especially when you're coming from so far away.

WANG MIAO

The MIDI festival is China's biggest gathering of alternative music, held over four days as summer comes to a close.

On 1 October 2005, Chinese National Day, I braved the streets around Tiananmen. Hundreds of thousands of patriots were heading to the square to pay homage to the People's Republic. It was a hot, fleshy day of pushing and shoving underneath a thick blanket of smog. The tunnels to the square were gridlocked; crowds grew anxious at the underground delays. Kids screamed and dropped their tiny red flags. The shells of fermented eggs crackled under step. The square itself absorbed the masses effortlessly, grand and grey, awash with spit and flapping flags.

Two days later I escaped to the festival in Haidian park, run by Beijing's MIDI School of Music. Stephen and I wandered the expanse of grass. Around the outside of the main area, stalls sold home-designed t-shirts, hats, badges, bootleg Japanese CDs, art magazines and a progressive youth identity. Everyone was a designer, trying to convert a hobby into a new brand. Boys lounged around in sunglasses exposing hairy nipples to the sunshine, smoking fags and primping 'fros. Girls tried on hippy skirts and tiny shorts (one with a furry Union Jack on the bum), and drank big plastic cups of beer. And there was that familiar sour scent of weed, especially near the loos and in the tent city on the slope. We loitered near the rugs that were spread out with stuff for sale, trying on hats. Stephen bought a very cool white and brown zip-up jacket. We then sat and ate *chuanr* and felt how wonderful it was to bask in the sunshine out of the choke of the city with a view of the Old Summer Palace. On this day, the western mountains enjoyed shades of blue rare in Beijing. Kites flew out long and deep, trying to reach them.

Stephen's best Chinese pal was a musician. Wang Miao was also becoming my friend, as my language improved. Wang Miao's band was called Sophie's Garden, a name taken from the book he never finished when he was 17 – *Sophie's World*, by Jostein Gaarder. An A-list underground band in its own right, Sophie's Garden had headlined all the major Beijing stages but had since split due to personality clashes. So even as an audience member at MIDI, Wang Miao was a modest celebrity. He knew the names and reputations of all the musicians on the main stage; they had gone to music school together: Convenience Store, Brain Failure, AK47.

He also came to the festival that day with a very pretty girl who was not his girlfriend.

Wang Miao and his actual girlfriend Jenny were one of Beijing's hottest, most volatile couples. Wang Miao was a drummer with voluminous yet sleek black-blue hair, a haughty pout normally reserved for catwalks, and an impressive range of clothes and bags. Wang Miao's smile would be calming if it wasn't also so handsome. It was for Wang Miao that the term *shuai* was invented. *Shuai* meant more than good-looking. It meant suave and knowing; more an attitude than a look.

I had met Wang Miao a month earlier. He was wearing aviator shades and had a curious habit of popping his mouth to make plosive sounds mid-conversation while clicking his fingers. I never questioned his coolness. Jenny was a talented classical flautist whose cat eyes took up most of her face; her smile filled the remaining space. Her dramatic makeup was impeccable, her long hair always shiny and well-conditioned. She liked frilly dresses and cute shoes. She had a flirt-mode that hinted at something powerful. The couple argued and split up time and time again. We never knew if they were together or not. One summer night, Wang Miao smashed a bottle against a wall outside Kai Bar in Sanlitun, spitting expletives on the broken glass. He then called all recently dialled numbers on Jenny's mobile, hunting down potential boy-threats. Jenny was no better. One night at another bar, she launched herself from a couch to attack a rival with claws flared. I saw the blood, and later, the scars.

Stephen and I wanted to cast the two melodramatists in a film. A story of music, the bad rock boy, the sweet classically trained girl, struggling against parental pressure and divergent life paths to stay together. We would set it in train yards, industrial parks and apartment stairwells. There'd be a tremendous amount of cigarette smoking.

Wang Miao chased Jenny for two years during high school. He says she 'thought I was kind of ordinary', and so he settled for a fraught friendship. But at the time he was enjoying being surrounded by like-minded musicians at his arty high school. His parents – not quite understanding his love of music – had bought him a piano accordion. Small, 13-year-old Wang Miao with his big accordion was an image I cherished.

'My parents didn't know how I hated that instrument – it was really, really big!' he exclaimed. Eventually, he was convinced by a mate to take up the drums. 'I've always liked music, so I've always wanted to be in a band.'

He called Jenny every day. 'We'd go out and have fun,' he remembers. 'Eat food, watch films, chat, go to the park.' Then came the day of breathless reckoning. 'She came to my house and I told her that I liked her then I gave her some flowers and a card that read "together forever".'

And so it started, the love affair whose tumult we were all subject to. Jenny had already graduated and Wang Miao's senior school was in a neighbouring province, so their time was romantically and torturously limited. 'Every Friday night I would finish study at six and hurry into Beijing,' says Wang Miao. 'She would be waiting for me in the McDonald's right near her house. But from Hebei to Beijing it took two hours! We'd be together only for the weekend. We'd hold hands the whole time. Sunday afternoon I would have to go back to Hebei. Every time she would say goodbye, every time she would cry at the bus stop.'

But still they fought like scrappy cats. 'We were really young and inexperienced and we'd break up at any problem,' Wang Miao told me. When they broke up, they kissed other people. They both had many people on the waiting list, some possibly just to get a glimpse of those famous cheekbones. 'I've had a lot of opportunities, but I've never slept with anyone else,' Wang Miao says.

Wang Miao made money from Sophie's Garden, not much, but it was around 100 kuai (£8) each for the four members for every show. To support the band Wang Miao worked at an internet advertising company and had another shit job selling apartments to rich people in the SoHo complex of tall white Lego-like buildings in the CBD. Yet he never had money. He was always asking Stephen for cash, even after appearing with a new manbag, and a mobile phone pendant that set him back 400 kuai.

With Sophie's Garden, Wang Miao had wanted to make it big, but the other three members were happy to keep things as they were. He thought they were slackers. That summer Wang Miao would target foreigners outside Beijing Culture and Language University trying to spot talent for his new band. 'Foreigners have a better attitude to music,' he said. I declined an offer to join as keyboardist. He also wanted Jenny in the band, playing flute. That's if they could stay together long enough to rehearse.

Haidian park was cold by the time Jenny met us after MIDI. We had just split with Stephen after dinner, and in a taxi heading home, I was chatting away in the front passenger seat. Having had no response for a while, I turned around to see Jenny and Wang Miao, mouths locked together and bodies pressed into the corner of the back seat.

I picked up my phone and called Stephen. 'Hello?' he said.

'It's back on,' I informed him. Cheekbones clashed in the background.

'Christ,' he said. 'Here we go again.'

CHAPTER 9

SUMMER DAYS

Across the road, beside the man selling plastic bags of assorted dried fruit and nuts, is the man that makes my favourite Beijing breakfast, *jian bing*.

I join a short queue for the popular egg pancake. The man uses a steaming round hotplate. In a fluid series of movements, he ladles pancake mixture onto the plate, takes a tool that looks like a window squeegee from a small bucket of water and swirls the mixture over the plate, a perfect circular motion, until it reaches the edges.

He cracks an egg into the centre and repeats the motion until the yolk and white infuse the pancake. The best part now: he flips it like a magic trick.

First he adds a sauce that tastes a little like soy, or Vegemite, or *hoisin* sauce; a dark jammy substance of fermented wheat, soy beans, sugar and chilli. It's a common accompaniment to *kao ya*, or Beijing Duck. The sauce is painted onto the pancake with a household paintbrush. He then asks *'Lai la jiao ma?'* Do I want chilli? I do but only a little, and he scoops up a thick-pitted paste, a deep puce colour, and mixes it with the brown sauce. The smell is mouth-watering.

He shakes black sesame seeds onto chopped spring onions and lots of coriander. On top of this he places a sheet of deep-fried dough waffle, and folds the pancake around it. The crispy wheat dough is broken in two places by the spatula, and the whole package is folded and put in a steaming plastic bag for two and a half kuai (about 20p). That, and a banana haggled from the market next door, is my perfect Beijing breakfast.

A humid and horny afternoon in Beijing has wound its spell of complete distraction. I am working the weekend shift tomorrow, so I'm sprawled on my bed in a pair of cotton boxer shorts waiting for Chinese Prince Awesome to come to my window and spare me the rest of Friday with a princely round. In lieu of Chinese Prince Awesome, I'm noodling texts to potentials, the objects of fantasised, hedonistic flings. A classic Leo, a proud, studly boy with a smile would be good. Into me in every way, but kinda dumb. That would do the trick.

I need to get out of the house. But it's an obstacle course of hipster students out there. What's a boy in summer to do? I thought this stopped with adolescence. But it seems only to get more needy. These days I have more specific desires: this combination of sandals and jeans, the hair and eyebrow combo, the killer one-two of a smile and a handshake. Thoughts rush to Nick – *it's just three hours' difference* – and I grab the phone for our daily chat, but hearing his voice will make me feel worse so I stop dialling and start getting dressed. I can't keep conjuring him like this. Like the heatwave, something must break. Would I leave China without learning anything new about love? Other than that it sucks to live without it?

So. I get out of the house. The hours between the end of the school day and dinner are the most fun in Beijing, especially in the summer sun. Teens in tracksuits double on bicycles and stampede into shops for confectionery and Cokes. There's forward movement everywhere. People are released. Boyfriends and girlfriends kiss on streets.

I join one flock heading into a park near the Drum and Bell Towers, then it's across the Second Ring Road to my favourite park in Beijing, Rendinghu Gongyuan.

A Greek pavilion is the park's welcome. Beyond it is a terraced rose garden. A hollowed-out piano, keys browned and jangly, sits underneath Aphrodite, pert atop her white column. Behind Greece BC is a Soviet fountain structure of copper and tiling. A series of elevated bridges take you past a mosaic of the capital's urban plan. Further on is a fantastical water park of slides and interconnected pools, which in early summer are still dry, revealing pipes. A menagerie of primary-coloured concrete animals would, I imagine, sprout water from their heads. Their eyes now look haunted by children's play.

Up further, at the top of the park, it is as if I have journeyed to the future: six brown mushroom-like sculptures are topped by long, slender spires. Kites have been caught on the Kubrick spires and hang there now like dead moths. Zooming around underneath, helmeted kids in electric toy cars compete.

It's so very unlike Beijing. There's a calm out the back. Grandfathers send up kites on that one gust of wind. Seniors in wheelchairs sit for an afternoon in the regenerating sun before they are inspected and collected by carers and cousins.

The grass is freshly green and long. There is a woman singing opera around the colonnades, her daily exercises. School students trade cards. Mothers come home from work with vegetables sticking out of string bags. It's expansive, green. I take up a whole bench while craving lying on the grass as I would in Sydney. I nap in the long afternoon light and wake reddened.

I walk back out through the park to join the activity of Beijing twilight. It's a time when families reunite and a game is struck, while someone finishes off the shopfront repairs and water begins its boil. I witness this great enterprise, a city talking, moving. I'm enlivened. I want to cheer at the people power, the pedal power.

Soon everyone will eat, and that will mark the beginning of the quiet that will last until morning.

At night-time the city looks like *Blade Runner*, all overpasses and apartment farms. Soon all of Beijing will look like the 'SoHo' complex where Wang Miao worked, built on the flat expanse southeast of Tiananmen Square. It comprises fifteen minimalist towers, angled towards each other to create the effect of a dense, discreet city. Grass-roots traditional courtyard houses are being pulled up like weeds, with hundreds of thousands displaced into vertical middle-class apartments – like a cross between the personality-free order of Zurich and the gigantism of Chicago. Since 2002, there has been more than 1.7 billion square feet of new construction in the multibillion-dollar pre-Olympic spending spree.

In the space of a week, gangs of migrant wreckers lay waste to the popular Sanlitun bar district. One of the city's 10,000 construction sites is a new shopping complex along Sanlitun North Street that looks like a prolapsed hotel bathroom: boxy chrome on the outside, and ribbed with mirrors.

The city is pouring concrete over memory. The pursuit of the future is evident in the net of cranes against the horizon, the nocturnal jackhammers, the restaurants entered along ramps, the solitary old guy who won't move from the now-abandoned dust bowl.

Not one thing is formed completely. One site to the east spans ten city blocks and contains nineteen cranes. The construction spills rubble; witches' hats delineate new temporary roads, and migrant workers, spades over shoulders, eat noodles on the curb. Another site contains twenty identical 28-storey apartment blocks built along an artificial water causeway. The windows are all empty, waiting for inhabitants.

The tension between old and new makes me anxious. But it speaks: *Get up and work, work, work*. China demands progress like no other country. It's doing what America did fifty years ago, but faster, with more ambition, and with more American entrepreneurialism than could ever fit behind an American picket fence.

A German consultant to the Chinese Ministry of Construction, Falk Kagelmacher, told me that when he worked in Berlin he designed city buildings to last 150 years, with maintenance costs built into the city's lifespan. In Beijing, he told me, buildings are built with a fifteen-year life cycle. In China's labour economy, where raw materials and migrant workers are cheap and abundant, it's more cost-effective to rip down the buildings and put up new ones than to maintain them. German architects take one and a half years to design a new building. Here it is six weeks. 'The building quality you see is just bad because of the sheer speed which is under way right now,' said Kagelmacher.

'The education is not bad here, technically it's good,' he said when we met for a coffee in the heart of Sanlitun's destruction. 'The deficiency is in thinking broadly. At first I thought it was bad, because the buildings fall apart in a few years. Now I think it's not that bad, because in China you cannot plan for the next ten years. So you don't *want* to have a building that lasts one hundred years, it's better that it falls apart.'

China does, then thinks. Spends, before it saves. The pace is so quick it makes working out this country difficult for a boy taught to look before he leaps and think before he speaks.

There was one refuge still, tucked down the dirty *hutong* past the drug-pushers and lady-bars in Sanlitun. A Friday night at the Kai bar – what Stephen and I called 'the inevitable'. We'd been there nearly every Friday night so far that summer.

Kai was a tiny venue, popular for ultra-cheap drinks and good dance music. Downstairs, bartenders struggled to keep up with the demand for poorly mixed gin and tonics. A packed but vibrant dance floor ringed a central silver pole. A heavily made-up prostitute would play with the necktie of a fat Westerner, while American college students lost their pole-dancing virginity to the whoops and malicious encouragement of onlookers.

Upstairs, free sofas were in short supply and the art gallery seemed – like the rest of the city – choked by pollutants and turning grey. At the height of summer, crowds spilled into the alleyways; hook-ups happened in the darker corners where blokes also pissed.

People from the embassies, the consulting companies, the English schools and the universities all indulging in Beijing's one occupational hazard: the need to get trashed on a Friday night.

One Friday night was the best of the 1980s. A tall, shaved-headed girl called Miao Miao was imitating Grace Jones in front of a mirror, knees marching high. She was wearing a floor-length black dress with bangles and red shell necklaces that hung down her flat chest. She was thin with no hips. She was beautiful.

I sipped on a hideously sweet cocktail mystery-ordered from the manager. 'It's too sweet,' I told him. 'I want it really sour.' He poured in half the lemon juice bottle, until it was an overripe glass of dance-power. It took me to where I wanted to go.

I saw black eyes come through the doorway, followed by the flash of white teeth. Jason turned up around midnight. He was wearing a baseball cap and had silver chains around his neck. His t-shirt read 'I am a virgin' in big letters and, in smaller letters underneath, 'this is an old t-shirt'. He whispered something in a friend's ear before picking his way through the crowd dancing to 'Sweet Dreams' by the Eurythmics. 'Hey,' he said. Then he told me to follow him through the *hutong* bends, my hand in his. We stopped at a roller door next to what looked like a hospital. He put his hand on my stomach under my t-shirt. It was the first time we had touched like this.

'I don't want a boyfriend,' I said.

'Me neither,' he replied. 'I just finished something big.'

'Me too. Really big. Still going.'

'So.'

We found it difficult to talk. I drew circles on his pale brown palms and looked around. Next to the hospital was some public exercise equipment. An old woman rotated her arm around a yellow-handled wheel. She moved in private thought to a red calf-massaging machine, which looked like a meat tenderiser set on a rolling pin.

'That's the problem with China,' Jason broke the silence.

'What's that?'

'Way too many fuckin' people,' he said, and kissed me.

'And too many teeth,' I complained.

He stuck out his tongue.

'Like this.' I kissed him back, swapping top and bottom lips. His piercing clinked against my teeth. 'Better.'

I felt worry slip away, replaced by a welcoming space of thoughtless desire. Cars could have passed, people on bikes, the old woman. He kissed my eyelids and looked me straight in the face. It was too much. His friends would be waiting.

'I'm sorry about turning up by myself and hanging around until you arrived,' I said. 'I know that that can suck.'

'It's fine,' he said.

'Should I stay?'

'Look at you, you're tired. What's happened to my Frodo?'

'Shut up.'

'Go home to sleep, I'll spend Sunday with you . . . Wait, James.'

He came over to where I had strayed in to say goodbye. I didn't want to be seen to be loitering, demanding.

'I told my friend I liked you,' he said. 'My friend said not to be a heartbreaker, Jason. Do you think that?'

'You, a heartbreaker?' I said, hopeless. A cart carrying empty water-cooler bottles skated past in silhouette. It was me that would be the heartbreaker, I thought, whenever that came around. Why can't desire run everything else as well as it runs itself?

This daggy guy, cool jeans. Chinese Prince Awesome? He looked like a skinny alien thug in his big t-shirt. He had a narrow waist. I ran my fingers up his hairless chest. He kissed me again and it almost became another event. 'Give me a hug,' he said. He smelled of cigarettes, the smell of my clothes and the taste of the inside of my mouth.

I left in a cab and turned up my headphones until they hurt my ears, trying to block out the world with music rather than kisses. But I couldn't.

Smog made the streetlights wear halos. This archangel city.

I didn't want my sense of belonging to be tied to a boy. I was bigger than that. I loved Nick.

I punched the seat. I wanted to take it back. But then I wanted to tell Jason to come over right now. To rip his clothes off and bite him and forget his name, forget Nick. Nick would be hurt. Pictures of him lurched through my head, weeping wives. My heart throbbed in my ears, the sound of regret.

Back home, I buried myself deep into my blanket, trying to forget. I lit up and sucked in a lungful of smoke and held. Pause. Exhale. I felt the tingling wash over my face to the back of my head and down my arms like soft-winged insects finding rest. I smoked the whole thing, lulled finally into sleep where I dreamed I was in Australia, on holidays up the coast, and someone had died and I was late for the funeral.

The summer heatwave did break and I found a clear Sunday afternoon to stroll lakeside in an area I had just discovered. Houhai – a Beijing-spit away from the ancient timepieces of the Drum and Bell Towers – was one of the city's most active and historic areas. The buildings here were between 200 and 300 years old. Hawkers, barbers and game-players took up seats along the kilometre of water. By day, the pathways around the imperial lakes became lovers' lanes. One hundred boys stared love-famished into the two hundred eyes of their girlfriends. Fat men swam in the shallow water.

I caught a rickshaw away from the lake down Nan Luo Guo Xiang, a stone alley lined with second-hand clothing stores, boutique bars that televised soccer, and a busy youth hostel. It trilled with bicycles and *hutong* hubbub. Fold-out plastic tables and chairs spilled around a small Xinjiang restaurant. I stopped in for a meal of home-style Uyghur food. Inside was a wall-sized poster: 'Mecca's Great Mosque'. Plastic grapes dangled from the ceiling. A dutiful son in a dirty white smock and white embroidered hat served me.

Dad, I presume, sweated over an active grill. His specialty was *∂a pan ji* (big plate chicken), a steaming earthenware pot of chicken and potato chunks in a spicy, wet sauce with wide, handmade noodles. Barbecued herb bread soaked up the rest of the sauce, and a round of lamb skewers finished things off.

Po lianr! Po liaaanrr! Outside I heard a weathered pedal-pusher drone for recycling. I saw commotion erupt when a man pulling a palm tree in a trailer ran into a teenager tinkering with the hanging of a new door. Two women with umbrellas were caught in the huddle. The scene ended with joking and backslapping. Some men helped the women cross the rubble.

The Xinjiang restaurant became a favourite of mine and at the end of each dinner there, I would count the empty bottles of Tsingtao as little achievements towards happiness.

In the evening, I drank beer in the Pass By Bar with my current lover, the one I always returned to, my laptop. Around me, genial Beijingers caught up before another busy week.

I felt my first surge – powerfully – of belonging. I didn't want to hoot. I smiled instead. That week I had abandoned my search for the authentic China, and let myself drift across a number of groups and new friends, with an ease I hadn't felt for a long time.

When dark came, Houhai shimmered with boat-lamps and blurred with booze. I sat to watch the middle-aged couples gather for mass ballroom dancing in the open air.

A dancer my mum's age overshot her twirl and swung right into me. Shocked, she collapsed in laughter and grabbed my wrist. '*Lai, lai, lai!*' she ordered. Come, come, come!

'No!' I protested but it was no use and she dragged me into a dance choreographed by a militant woman with a boom box.

She poked me in the stomach and grinned like a mad person, '*Ni hen shuai,*' she said. I blushed. You're very handsome. Dizzy, we began. Hand on shoulder, spin, shuffle, step left, not right. 'Whoops!' Laughter.

Rotate, part, turn, hug and giggle.

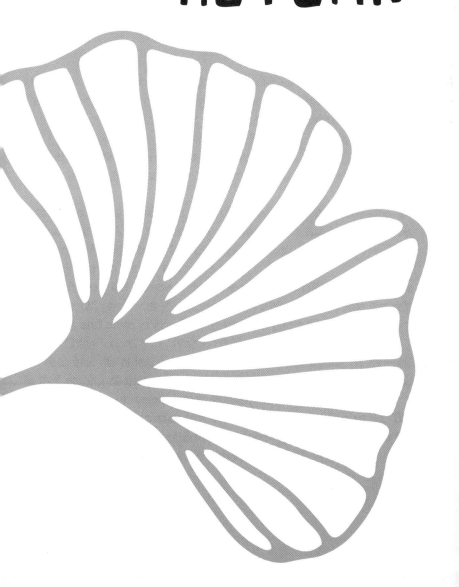

PART TWO

AUTUMN

CHAPTER 10

THE PRACTICAL ONES

'You killed your Aborigines,' says Wang Xiaoke over fish hot pot. We are in the China Radio International restaurant. Waiters have seasonal outfits here – autumn requires full-length purple velveteen. CRI management drink *baijiu* and smoke around circular tables.

Wang Xiaoke has provided my first real chance to get at what the West has made Asian fetish. The Big China Bads: human rights abuses, organ trade, Tibet, forced labour camps for Falun Gong practitioners, the state-led hatred of Japan.

I wanted to know what young Chinese felt about their country; there were, after all, more than 200 million Chinese aged between 15 and 24. I wanted to see it through Wang Xiaoke's eyes, as a peer. I wanted to be different from the old expats blithely listing China's crimes like mantra while fucking China's women. That was a China cliché. I wanted nuance.

Wang Xiaoke was a radio announcer and my first Chinese friend. She gave me my Chinese name after weeks of careful thinking. Wei Si Jie. The first part was like 'West' and meant 'kingdom', among other things. The second part meant 'quick thoughts'. I was touched.

She had a cute, mousy face with alert eyes and a bemused smile. She walked like a tomboy, giggled like a girl, and wore overalls with high-top sneakers. I thought she was brave. She thought I was a kid.

She signed my stationery registers and booked my cars. She arranged my shifts with bosses. I helped her with her weekly business programme and entertained her across cubicles. She documented my morning tiredness with daily snapshots. She gave me regional Chinese snacks that looked like lollies. It never got old for her, that look on my face when I discovered they were meat, not sweet, and ran for the bin.

The conversation over fish hot pot had started after I found another blocked website, the Human Rights Watch. The government had blocked websites at its nine gateways using technology bought from companies like Cisco; BBC, parts of CNN, Wikipedia, and elements of Google were filtered. Rebecca MacKinnon, formally the CNN Beijing bureau chief, now teaching new media at Hong Kong University, says that China's blogger population exploded to ten million in 2005. 'It was China's Year of the Blog,' MacKinnon joked in an interview later in Hong Kong. The boom led to even tighter controls.

'Companies have to obey the censorship laws in order to stay in business,' Rebecca MacKinnon told me, 'in order not to be shut down.' Companies hired more staff and bought filtering systems designed to flag problematic posts for follow-up or automatic deletion.

Mostly though, censorship is about the reader, says MacKinnon. Its sole purpose is to guard against a critical number organising around one issue. 'An emerging Chinese [Ahmed] Chalabi, that's the last thing they want,' she said.

When the popular blogger Michael Anti called for a boycott of the *Beijing News*, after authorities fired the editorial staff and more than one hundred staff walked out, his blog was shut down. 'Bloggers with big readerships are going to get found,' MacKinnon explained.

No Michael Anti, I was still kicked off the internet several times. Had one of the 30,000 internet police finally decided I had reached my quota of searches on risky subjects? Once, an MSN chat with a friend about sex was cut short just as the better adjectives started flying. That outage lasted twenty-four hours. That was random, considering porn was plentiful.

I tell Wang Xiaoke about proxy servers and how to get through the Great Firewall, which irritates her. 'Why do you want to access these websites anyway?' she asks. 'Everyone accepts that access also means a certain level of restriction. Freedoms mean certain laws.'

'They're denying millions of people the right to know,' I say. Wang Xiaoke's arched eyebrow capitalises my comment: The Right to Know.

I find myself talking in capitals a lot around Wang Xiaoke.

'We have our own problems just like you do, Jimmy-boy, and we are working them out, slowly,' she says. 'People here have always followed what people from above tell them. We don't question it. We accept it. But slowly people are thinking about these things, lots of people right across China. But what power have we had? You come from a democracy. You killed your Aborigines, and what was that boat that you turned around, the *Tampa* or something?'

Wang Xiaoke is proud of China. Why wouldn't she be? She is, with her generation, about to inherit China. I kept encouraging Wang Xiaoke to make her talents known to the BBC or CNN. 'You could do anything, Wang Xiaoke. You're talented.'

'This is my job,' she replied. 'Sometimes I hate it, but it's what I have.'

I had this feeling I couldn't shake that Wang Xiaoke was actually despondent. She appeared to be living her generation's dream, but something had gone wrong along the way. Something had gone wrong with the dream itself.

Wang Xiaoke was ambitious. Ambition, she knew, would get her out of the tiny copper-mining town in the south, home for seventeen years, and into the moneymaking jobs of the north.

She studied international economics and trade. 'It's hot,' she says, 'with the Chinese economy booming.' Wang Xiaoke grew up in Dongxiang, a mining town with 1,000 employees, two of whom were her parents. The state-owned Jiangxi Copper Company ran seven mines in Jiangxi province including Wang Xiaoke's home-town, which became the largest copper production base in China, yielding a fifth of the country's supplies.

Without the shackles of the planned economy that had kept her parents in the mine *danwei* (the work unit), and without the Cultural Revolution restrictions, Wang Xiaoke belonged to a generation that could finally choose. Her exit plan was assured on graduating from high school. Today nearly nine million high school students annually sit the National University Entrance Exam (the be-all and end-all three-day *gaokao*), where a small point difference in results can mean very different life paths. During my year in China, accord-ing to government numbers, there were only 2.6 million college places up for grabs. But simply getting into college wasn't enough for Wang Xiaoke in 1997. She wanted a seat at one of the capital's prestigious institutions.

Degrees were coveted keys to top jobs, but perhaps surprisingly, a pursuit also justified by spirituality. University education was fundamental in the Confucian path of social advancement. Wang Xiaoke made the cut and moved to Beijing for the competitive pro-gramme in economics at Beijing Normal University. The university ranked third in China for social sciences. 'Not as good as Beijing University,' she says, 'but still pretty good.'

Wang Xiaoke excelled, especially in English competitions, which were high-profile events. Some of these were big, inter-var-sity showdowns, some were televised and government ministers attended. They were cruising grounds for corporate headhunters looking to seduce the brightest star with the best job. Wang Xiaoke was picked up by a foreign-backed recruitment agency straight out of university.

'Did you enjoy university?' I ask her.

'What's not to enjoy?' says Wang Xiaoke.

'Well, some people don't like study, I guess,' I say.

'Nup. Not me.' She leans back in her chair. 'I was carefree.'

'Yeah, but that's because you were living away from your parents.'

'Oh alright, OK,' she laughs. 'That was the major reason. Selfish, huh?'

'Naw. Why do you say selfish?'

'My parents always think about me. I only think about myself.'

I tell Wang Xiaoke I'm the reigning champion 'Worst Son Ever'.

'Bet that's not true.'

'About as true as you being selfish.'

Chinese universities were tough. Not like my spliff-hazy days spread-eagled on the grass at the University of Sydney. There, we lolled around the edges of student protests, fashionably uncommitted. A liberal education. Very liberal, aimed at making me well-rounded. There was a cultural expectation of activism. So much so, it made most eyes glaze over: subvert the dominant paradigm; counterculture is our engine for change; youthful idealism isn't naive, it's innovative; resistance is itself a creation of power. Thanks Foucault.

For Chinese students, though, getting into university didn't mean they could breathe out (by breathing in illegal substances). It was only the beginning. Once inside, competition was fierce because the students were packed in like sardines. Since the 1977 reinstatement of the *gaokao* after the Cultural Revolution, college placements have soared. Where do all the students go? The answer: eight bunk beds per 20-square-metre dorm room.

'That's crowded,' I say to Wang Xiaoke.

'But it also made me feel close to everyone.'

'Physically! What about privacy?'

'What do you mean privacy?' Wang Xiaoke asks. 'What kind of privacy?' The Chinese word for privacy had similarities to 'secrecy'. Its connotation was mainly negative, selfish.

'Well, what happened if somebody wanted to bring home a boy-friend?'

'Usually we didn't. I think it's still very rare that college students would bring their boyfriends or girlfriends to their residence, especially on campus.'

'So where do they go?' I ask. Every afternoon, after school, two love-struck students I knew – unable to go home – rode the subway to the end of the line and had sex in the deserted lots near construction sites. A very Beijing love affair.

'I don't know where they go!' Wang Xiaoke exclaims. 'Outside the school! A hotel room! Is that what you mean? When I was in college, life was much simpler than now.'

In 1989, Wang Xiaoke's university was a hotbed of dissent. Beijing Normal University's students organised four teams of 500 students each to spend twelve-hour shifts in Tiananmen Square in the month before the tanks rolled in. Wuerkaixi, a 21-year-old education science student, led the groundswell of activism. He was a brilliant orator and famously appeared in a national broadcast in what looked like pyjamas (actually a hospital gown – he'd been admitted for an inflammation of the heart, a result of hunger strikes). He rebuked then-premier Li Peng for being a month late to the negotiation table, and he became a star. Beijing Normal University students made the press. 'If we get our immediate goals – including a dialogue with the government – we will calm down a bit and be able to study. But our movement won't be over,' one Beijing Normal University activist told the Associated Press days before the massacre. Of course, the movement did die, along with scores of students. The numbers vary depending on who's giving them – from the hundreds to several thousand. A week after the slaughter, the Public Security Bureau of Beijing, via the state press, issued a most-wanted circular for the arrest of twenty-one student leaders for 'inciting and organising counter-revolutionary rebellion'. Three were from Beijing Normal University, including Wuerkaixi, who fled to Taiwan.

In the intervening decade between Tiananmen and when Wang Xiaoke graduated in 2000, campus activism had vanished. And no one talks about the Square. 'Some students still have very strong political ideas nowadays, but not too many I guess,' Wang Xiaoke wrote to me later. 'One thing for sure is that competition is fiercer and college students work harder and are more pragmatic than the students in the 1980s and early 1990s.'

It wasn't the last time I would hear the word 'pragmatic' used to describe this Chinese generation.

But Tiananmen hasn't been totally struck from consciousness. 'So do you think China should talk about it?' I ask Wang Xiaoke.

'I think so. There's no history that cannot be talked about.'

'There's a lot of Chinese history that has not been talked about.'

'Yeah. I know. For you. Have you ever done something and you didn't want others to know about it – have you ever had this experience?'

'Ha. Yeah,' I shrug. 'All the time.'

She pauses then leans forward and asks, 'But for a country it's different, right?'

Did young Beijingers really have no memory? Did pragmatism dictate a new politics of individuality and materialism? Andy, 25, was a Chinese editor and producer for state-run television. He was eight years old and in Beijing during the massacre.

His clearest memory of that time was being sent home from school for two weeks. His school was worried about security. It was a holiday for Andy. He was too young to understand the shifts the protests meant to a government trying to install stability for the next decades of economic growth. Now, he didn't care. It was another time, another place. 'It's like there's this force to forget,' he said. 'You want to forget.'

Nan Luo Guo Xiang was an apt place to interview Andy, itself in the grip of a generational gear-change. The *hutong* was slated for renovations. One dwelling that looked like Bilbo's hobbit home had lost its roof in the last week. In one day a French-inspired restaurant had lost its façade; a tableau of a functioning restaurant could still be seen within. Over the next few months I would watch the road widen and be repaved, the shopfronts 'restored', people moved out. There would be no old women in pyjamas reading newspapers. We would see an increase in rent and rickshaw tours. The Xinjiang restaurant would, thankfully, remain.

Andy and I ordered coffee, not tea, and ate bacon and eggs.

'Politics can't compete with opportunity,' said Andy. He was a tall, serious boy; expressions rarely cracked his porcelain-like face.

'Very, very few people care about politics,' he said. 'I think most care about technology, business, lifestyle.' Andy himself had carved out a reputation at the station for heartfelt human-interest stories.

'I don't like politics that much,' he admitted. Ditto for his generation. 'People think that individuals can't change entire policies. And if you did make that effort you might get into trouble. Although I think that China is actually opening up a lot, compared to ten years ago, compared to my parents' time.'

I heard this time and again. It wasn't apathy. It was a disconnect from parental suffering and the magnitude of the political machine. It was a way to make a new identity. It explained the brand-worship, the mall-hopping, the KFC-dating: a way to divorce from the past and look to the future.

Popular blogger Beijing Loafer, aka Hao Wu, summed it up. 'Between ideology and consumer culture, I'd choose the latter any day.

'China appears to have too much baggage on its shoulder[s] – history, nationalism, glory and despair,' he continued on his blog, Beijing or Bust. 'It's liberating to see young people able to live freely, unlike the older generations, able to live for themselves without the burden of memories for once.'

'What happened in 1989 was beamed everywhere around the world,' I told Andy. 'But nobody my age, no one who is 23 or 24 seems to know what happened.'

'How did you know about it?' Andy asked.

'I was seven and I still remember the footage,' I said. 'As a kid I knew nothing about China and very little about the world. But those images stayed in my head: the tanks rolling down the street and the man with the flag. That was the first thing I knew about China.'

'But you also remember stories about other countries who were having the same problems?' Andy prodded, his thin eyebrows arching.

'Not as much, to be honest,' I said. 'I don't have much memory of international news apart from that incident. But then here, no one knows about it, no one talks about it.'

Andy says what I'm seeing is a result of powerlessness. 'The system that runs the whole country is like this. I don't want to do anything to help this change.' He held his pale hand to his chest. 'I don't think this one small person can change the whole system. So maybe that's why a lot of people like me don't think they can change a thing.'

CHAPTER 11

HOW TO
BE YOUNG

'My parents are a different breed, and sometimes we can't communicate,' says 19-year-old Zi Xiang. He has wide, thin eyes and his pointy face is battling a nasty round of acne. 'My parents and I don't agree about what clothes to wear, and where to go out for fun.'

Beijing Gong Nue (Beijing Strategy), one of the rabbit warrens in Xidan shopping mall, is a marketplace of identities for the post-Mao, post-Tiananmen kids. Here you can be anything you choose to buy. Zi Xiang is lanky and stands out in the maze of stalls that sell watches, sunglasses, bangles, rings, necklaces, scarves, mobile phone holders and trinkets. Music thumps. Light refracts through fake diamonds and reflects off Zi Xiang's silver earrings. After classes finish, this place swarms with people like him.

His new Nokia mobile phone cost 3,800 kuai (about £310), nearly twice the average monthly income for a Beijinger. He gets his money from his father, who owns a real estate company, then shows off his fashionable mullet in the multi-storey clubs along the west of the Workers' Stadium – Mix, Babyface, Cargo – where the drinks are expensive and the attitudes exhausting. 'I drink a lot, and I always get drunk.'

There's an assumption about the young in Beijing. They aren't ready. They're irresponsible. They're apathetic. They don't deserve to inherit a country. It's said that a generation with no memory of struggle has no respect for tradition. Those now in their 20s – students, and those starting careers – are too young to know about Tiananmen, and their parents' China is one that bears little resemblance to China today. This generation is the first to be handed the New China. And what are they doing with it? By all accounts, spending it on jeans.

'The generations have such different thoughts and ideas,' says Chen Chen, the 25-year-old manager of the Levis store in the mall next to Beijing Strategy. 'China is developing so fast at the moment and young people have very different and independent thoughts.' He holds his Nokia as he talks. He is dressed in a black peaked cap, a designer knit and adidas sneakers. His favourite film is *Trainspotting*.

Mobility has widened the generation gap. Literally. For many young people here, Beijing isn't home. They grew up as children of China's economic reform in newly industrialised cities in the south. They were coddled, they say – this generation made up of only children – by two decades of capitalism with Chinese characteristics. They were fed lines about opportunity through education. At last a generation had the money to dream of faraway places; they were drawn to the big, powerful cities on the coast. But in Beijing, there are no parents, and there's a terrible freedom.

Chen Chen furrows his brow and says the assumption that young people are swept away by money is not altogether true. 'I think the Chinese young generation is under great pressure now and a simple life is actually what we are looking for.' These Xidan shoppers feel the tension between tradition and their newfound freedom. They still long for security. Candy, 21, lowers her eyelids and admits her ideal husband will be 'nice to me, and have a good job'. Stocky Xu Jie, 20, shrugs and says he just wants to be 'healthy, honest and nice to my parents', even though they are 'a bit conservative and have different thoughts about money'.

Nisly, 20, is zipping up her bright pink jacket. She studies anthropology at the Central University for Nationalities and works as a translator at the Malaysian Embassy. Today she is also my translator. She knows there are generational differences, but says she is lucky because her parents are cosmopolitan. 'My parents are not so typical of Chinese parents. They are open-minded and fashionable too, so I've never had any big problems with them. But maybe they didn't agree when I had a boyfriend in high school because they thought it would affect my schoolwork.' Nisly's dad has his own business, and her mum is a housewife. She gets 6,000 kuai a month (about £490) from her job, and then an extra 2,000 kuai pocket money from her family, which she calls 'more than enough'.

But the money-spending phase will come to an end. As they grow older, many will be absorbed into compulsory marriage and secure jobs. 'I'll get married after 30. I'm not ready for marriage yet,' says Chen Chen. He pulls a cigarette from his shirt pocket, tucks it behind his ear. 'People here are still kind of traditional. It's not as if I can do what I want. There are many things I need to do to be prepared for marriage, like a good job, a house or money.'

While some would argue that the opening economy has both created a poverty of idealism and turned a whole generation into shoppers, it has in fact created a new pragmatism, which is necessary to balance traditions such as marriage with the pressure to overachieve.

The China Youth and Children Research Centre says pressure starts young and continues throughout early adulthood. High-school students spend over fourteen hours a day on schoolwork. Part-time classes take up most of their weekends and holidays. Two-thirds of Beijing high-school students signed up for part-time classes during winter break. In one survey, a third of high-school students felt pressured by their parents. Little wonder: 90% of parents said they expected their kids to get degrees, and over a half said they expected their children to get PhDs. Then, there's *marriage*.

'Oh, mother!' moaned Andy over our breakfast in Houhai. He raked his fingers through his thick mop of black hair and scrunched up his nose at me. 'Oh, I can tell you stories!'

Andy was raised by his mother. From a young age he was pressured to be different, to get better marks, and success was too important to be simply left to Andy; teachers regularly endured audiences with his mum.

'I hated that,' Andy said. 'I didn't like to be treated differently from other classmates.'

The defining experience of Andy's parents' early adulthoods was the Cultural Revolution. 'Both of them lived through that period in the 1950s. They went through a lot. Both of them are serious people as a result. It's rare to hear any jokes from them. It's really, really hard. I was taught to be serious. There were lots of rules. I think that's because my father was from the army.'

Andy's parents were strangers when they married; it was an arrangement made by their mothers and aunts. 'It wasn't a solid foundation for their marriage,' Andy reflected. When Andy was a kid, his father was in the People's Liberation Army and studying French to become a Chinese diplomat in Paris. He then chose career over family as a military attaché in Chinese embassies around the world. Andy became the sole focus of his mum's attention.

'As my mother gets older she's afraid of letting me go because I'm all she has. My father's always travelling,' he said. 'Occasionally she gets angry with me for not going home often enough. When you have one child in your family, like most post-1980 children, it's hard.'

Andy followed his mum's education strategy, and completed a degree from one of the nation's best universities. But he'd had enough of being programmed to succeed. He turned down postgraduate study in Los Angeles for this TV gig, against his mum's wishes. Working for a top-notch outlet was a clear road to the top of Beijing's media pack. Successful employees enjoyed street cred and PR perks.

Andy could now distance himself from family. His dad would have paid his US tuition, but that meant more strings. 'I didn't want to depend on my father.' Andy recrossed his legs. 'I did it for myself.'

He chose to live in the run-down station dormitories rather than his middle-class family home in the old Dongcheng district. 'I can manage my own life,' he had told his mum.

'I would dream about working for a television station when I was in middle school,' Andy remembered. 'I listened to rock music, pop music, Western music. I was quite influenced by it.' Now, at 25, Andy helps run a national music programme with an audience of millions. He is confident, and lovely to work with; he puts people at ease with compliments. 'At my age I know it's something that a lot of people dream of,' he said. 'So I really cherish what I'm doing now.'

But not Mum. She has accepted Andy's position but is busy making other plans for him. The latest scheme is Project Marriage. 'Every time I go home for the weekend,' Andy groaned, 'I'm afraid she will start "the conversation", saying, "OK, so tell me about your girlfriend? You must have a girlfriend!" I don't want to get married. I'm not refusing marriage, if the time is right. But I don't know now.'

Andy is stuck, like a lot of his generation, between ambition and tradition. And the emotional estrangement that follows this creates 'secrets'. Andy started keeping secrets. Big, whopping secrets not even his friends knew about. The one thing most apparent to me about the painful generation gap in China was the lack of honesty.

Andy's slender fingers selected a spoon and stirred sugar into his coffee. 'It's something I feel like talking to you about because I think it's going to help your book.'

Andy did have a girlfriend. She was in another province. And married. She had a child. The unconventional affair had lasted two years in whispers and business trips. Did her husband know? 'I think he suspects,' said Andy, 'but he doesn't have the proof.'

He blinked several times then hid behind his hair. 'I'm so tired. I just want get out of this thing. But emotionally it's hard to make a decision with someone you have already spent two years with. You know, all that energy and investment. She is beautiful,' he sighed, showing his face again. 'But I've never met the kid. And it's already been two years; I don't know how long I can last.'

Work gives Andy stability. He has been at the station for four years but won't stay forever. He wants to host a children's TV programme then see rest of the world, once he sorts things out with his girlfriend and his mother. In five years what will he be doing? 'Learning journalism. Helping poor kids to study. I'm thinking of working on my own project, but I haven't figured it out yet.'

I interrupt him. 'You know, I wonder from time to time if you're OK.' He looks up, surprised. 'I hope life isn't *too* serious for you.'

'Yeah, I know,' he nods and takes a short breath. He rubs his face with both hands then smiles. 'When you get too serious, then you're not attractive.'

At CRI, Wang Xiaoke earns an above average wage, a respectable 6,000 kuai per month (about £490). That makes her well-off. She can save money; rent is a quarter of her income. She gives 2,500 kuai (about £200) to her parents every month, 'because they are living with me now, they take care of my stuff'.

'That's the reason behind giving your parents money every month?'

'Why else? It's because they raised me,' she says. 'But I think now, an increasing number of young people don't do it any more because they don't have enough to support themselves.'

Twenty-somethings care about jobs and the coveted Chinese work permit, the *hukou*. And for good reason: they're in short supply. According to the Ministry of Labour and Social Security, in 2006 about 1.24 million Chinese college students graduated to find jobs for which they were overqualified. Financiers work as bank tellers. Business majors work in retail. Audio technicians sell apartments.

Then twenty-somethings must confront the challenge to stay in the capital once studies have finished. Beijing residents automatically get a Beijing work permit, a remnant of the planned economy. In the famines of the 1950s and 1960s, the *hukou* helped ration and distribute food to administrative centres. If you moved, you needed to re-register to be entitled to resources from your new local government.

'You don't have to get it today,' explains Wang Xiaoke, 'but once you do, it's sort of like a US green card. It gives you privilege. For each university there are a limited number of *hukou* given to students. They only take the top three or five or ten.'

'So if you don't have a *hukou* in Beijing and you can still work, why did you want it?'

'For my children's education. To get better education.'

'So with a *hukou*, you can get into better schools?'

'Not really.'

'So why does this thing still exist?'

'It has a long history,' she says. 'People have this mindset that you have to get it. As you've seen, a lot of privileges are gone, so more and more Chinese don't care about the *hukou*. I know, I confuse you!'

'Did your parents want you to get it?'

'Yeah. It means stability. Really, it doesn't make any sense,' she shakes her head. 'State-run companies *used* to provide you with *hukou*. But the policy changed last year. They don't give you *hukou* anymore because people come and go so often.'

For some, deregulation has meant opportunities for many jobs in one lifetime. For others it's simply terrifying. China's population is ageing faster than the world's average and, unlike Western countries, it is getting older before it is getting richer. China's economy is carrying 300 million people into old age from its post-Great Leap Forward baby boom of the late 1960s. By 2050, a third of the population will be retirement age. The one-child policy has exacerbated the ageing effect on the economy. It means that one couple will support four parents into old age. For single children the pressure can be too much.

Hence there is a dark side to China's economic celebration. In the six months before I arrived in Beijing, fourteen students killed themselves in schools and universities. Suicide is the biggest killer of Chinese between the ages of 15 and 34, at a rate amongst the highest in the world, over twice that of Australians the same age. It's the worst in this age group – 20% of 140,000 high school students interviewed by Beijing University said they had thought about suicide – but it's also a cross-generational problem. A quarter of a million people kill themselves every year in China; it is the fifth leading cause of death for the total population.

Wang Xiaoke has noticed the rise in reporting suicide in China. 'I think the fundamental reasons are due to the radical changes in our society. It's just too much for people to handle. And when people are busy pursuing material wealth, unfortunately, they quite often neglect the building of their spiritual world. And I myself have a feeling that as more and more Chinese are exposed to individualism – a core value in Western society – as the country is opening up to the world and becomes increasingly "Westernised", people are eager to realise their individual values. I'm not saying it's a bad thing. But when people fail to realise self-defined values, *that's* the problem. And when people don't have a caring family member or friend to talk to, or a serene mind, mental illnesses are very likely to sneak in.'

'In 2004,' Wang Xiaoke tells me, 'I learnt that one of my schoolmates, who used to be the president of the student union, killed herself because of long-term depression after she was dumped by her boyfriend. She used to be so energetic, dazzling, so outstanding.'

Wang Xiaoke herself is not immune to feelings of unhappiness. Yet she's living the dream.

'For a Chinese student, a career course is really simple. Sometimes they just do a job for a living, just for a living. It's not their interest. They don't have plans. I'm one of them.'

'Huh?' I'm frustrated when she says things like this. 'Why do you say you're one of them?'

'Because you forced me to say it!' She flops back in her chair. 'Because I rarely ask myself why am I doing this, or what am I going to do next.'

'Come on. I don't think that's me forcing you to say that.'

'Yeah you do. You force me to think about it.'

'So what happened after university finished?' I redirect, but what I really want to ask her is what happened to her plans.

'What happened? CRI happened to me!'

Wang Xiaoke did want the security of the *hukou* and to stay in Beijing. So she sat an exam at CRI. Her first job was as a reporter. She loved it. 'You feel curious about everything, don't you? Everything's new. It feels good to learn something.' She learned how to write stories and how to edit audio, but soon realised she had restrictions.

'What else did you learn about the Chinese media that first year?' I ask.

'It's all about censorship!' Agitated, she shuffles in her chair.

'You're just saying that for me now.'

'No. You know what? I think it's true. There are a lot of forbidden areas, what things you can do, what things you cannot. You know that.'

'I know that.'

In 2004, Wang Xiaoke was chosen to work for Radio Australia, the ABC's international service. She lived in Melbourne and worked for twelve months for the Mandarin service. Colleagues said she came back more confident, more opinionated and more competent. She cut her hair, got new glasses. She was invigorated.

'There was no censorship,' says Wang Xiaoke. 'Of course, you have editorial policies, but as long as you follow the rules, you can talk about anything you like. You can interview whoever you want.'

'I imagine after your Melbourne experience, you would have seen things differently when you came back to CRI.'

'Yeah. The first couple of days, of course, you feel uncomfortable.'

'*Did* you feel uncomfortable?'

'What do you want me to say?' Wang Xiaoke asked. 'Yes. I felt uncomfortable.'

'In what way?'

'Look.' Suddenly she is serious. 'I would think, "How come I can't do this story? It's unreasonable that I'm not allowed." But then we're creatures of habit, and I just got used to it. Maybe I complained sometimes. But that's all I could do.'

Lunch is almost over. 'How does that make you feel now?'

She pauses. 'Numb.' There is a long silence and we look at each other as if from opposite sides of a galaxy. 'Do you feel sorry for me?' she says quietly.

'No. I don't feel sorry.'

'I feel insulted, because it's my right to talk about things, you know. Sometimes that right is taken away from me.'

For a moment I wish Wang Xiaoke had never been to Melbourne, but this is a patronising thought. Like all great travellers, she knew she'd never truly fit back in when she returned. When you first come back, everything seems unchanged and uninformed. And then, months later, you realise you're a completely, utterly different person.

The next day, Wang Xiaoke emailed me. 'I found a quote by Alexandre Dumas from *The Count of Monte Cristo*: "All human wisdom is summed up in these two words – wait and hope."'

CHAPTER 12
MY GUARD'S JACKET

Autumn was Beijing's best season. The sky looked like stonewashed denim, but the light faded by the day. Aeroplanes streaked the sky. Dryness made everything electric. It made my hair flat and my clothes crackly. Kissing a friend on the cheek was a shock of static you could hear. Closing a taxi door jolted you onto the street. Warm places were crowded and cold places became thoroughfares. The *ni* was dropped from *ni hao* unless indoors. Steam built up in display windows; noodle steam. Things were slowing down.

Heating was turned on by some unknown decree in early November above the Yangtze River, and a few weeks later below. I imagined small villages south of the river building fires in these weeks before coal coloured everything. At night, way up in the north it was already a shoulder-shaking cold. It gave me a strange sense of belonging to be part of a city of shiverers. I wrapped myself in blankets and wore jumpers to bed.

The city made more sense in autumn. People's watchfulness, their composed solitude, made more sense – the only defence against the weight of others.

I raced around the corner from Tiananmen East subway station up Nanchizi to find my guard.

He jumped out from the park onto the street in front of me, displaying his brand-new winter jacket. He grinned and spun on the spot twice. The jacket flared and caught the wind.

For two weeks I had been asking my guard where his jacket was; the others all had new jackets. Finally it arrived. A proper, full-length jacket, an inch thick, emblazoned with the red star and topped with a huge fur hood. He looked good. He was very happy and so was I.

We had become friends over the past month. His post was at the gate to the ornamental park that ran behind Chang'an Avenue and led to the main gate of the Forbidden City. He was 21. He was always pleased to see me. Head nods turned into hellos over a week then into a first, thrilling conversation for both of us. Now we chatted every morning and every night on my way to and from work. Sometimes I would stop by on the weekend and, against the rules, he would join me in the park, looking at the white bridge and the trees losing their leaves. We would talk or just sit and not say anything.

My guard knew my schedule better than me. One day, running to the subway, he shouted after me, 'You're late! You are always late! Your boss thinks you're lazy!' *Little do you know*, I thought. He laughed and laughed and ran after me. He poked his head around the corner to see me leap three steps at a time.

'My job is so boring,' my guard told me that evening. He was breaking sticks and throwing the bits into the canal. 'I am going home to Hubei province at the end of this month. My dad says I have a bad job.'

'That's terrible,' I said. 'I don't want you to go. I'll miss you every day. What will you do at home?'

'I don't know. My dad says it's no trouble. I like English. I like studying English.'

'Your English is excellent,' I said, but in truth, it wasn't very good. We conducted every conversation in Chinese. 'You can go to school?' I suggested.

'I don't have any money.'

'Before you go home to Hubei, we should go to a bar and drink beer. What do you reckon?'

He grabbed my shoulders. 'To a bar to drink beer?' He grinned. 'OK! That *is* a good idea.' He leapt up, grabbed a fistful of grass and threw it into the air. 'Drinking beer! Drinking beer!' The grass rained down. I laughed. But he stopped. 'I don't know where you live.'

'I live northwest of this street, you dumb egg,' I said, and crouched on the park bench to watch him make small piles of ripped grass. 'And you?'

He gave a description I didn't understand, but I thought it was something to do with a guard dormitory just down the road.

'A lot of people?' I asked.

'Yes, yes. Too many people!'

'That's the problem,' I said.

'What?'

'With China. There are always too many people. Your room-mates, are they nice?'

'Yes. I like them a lot,' he said but he wasn't listening. He was grabbing the bench and shaking it to unbalance me. 'Have you had dinner, small monkey?' he asked.

'Yes. I'm sorry,' I said, before I fell onto his back. He heaved me into a piggyback and ran down the hill towards the canal. He tripped and we fell on the grass.

'What time do you finish work today?' I gasped. 'Nine o'clock like yesterday?'

'Every day I finish at nine o'clock, you know that. Will I see you tomorrow?'

'Yes. After work I will come and see you,' I said. 'Next week, we'll get food?'

'Very good! See you tomorrow, Australian pal!' He let me go a few steps then reached out and grabbed my hand. 'Sleep well!'

I feel we are good friends, my guard and me. We have something in common, this struggle for language. God, I don't want him to leave. He is such a part of my life in Nanchizi. I never imagined he would leave before I did. I don't even know his name!

He has no email address, no phone, only a postal address in Hubei.

Maybe I will visit him and his schoolyard girlfriend, and meet his family for Spring Festival. Maybe I will help him with his English.

I wonder if he has to give that jacket back. It's a really nice jacket.

HAO WU

I read Hao Wu's blog, Beijing or Bust, every day. In the pack of Chinese bloggers writing in English, Hao was way out front. I wanted an insider's guide to China and Hao was there to help. I spent the day with him – a morning anecdote followed by an afternoon check-in. My colleagues knew Hao too. I imagined him to be an attractive, erudite Chinese man in his early 30s. He was educated in the West, and had an intimate knowledge of two cultures.

It wasn't only his charm that hooked me. In China I was attracted to gay characters as a way to chart a course through these strange waters, and not simply because I was gay. With their embodiment of the public-private split in China, gay people understood China's contradictions and displayed panache in juggling them without despair.

I like meeting my heroes, so I arranged to interview Hao in SoHo at one of Beijing's fifty-nine Starbucks cafés, because, Hao said on the phone, 'Where else can you find civilisation in Beijing?'

Hao's demeanour doesn't disappoint. He is reading *The Economist* and sipping a latte as I enter. He is wearing black-framed glasses and shiny lip balm. He has a round face with a high forehead and sparse eyebrows. 'So what do you want to talk about?' he asks when I throw my jacket over the sofa. He is busy, so after I introduce myself and record his biographical details, we launch into the big topics.

'Is the internet a democratising force in China?' I ask.

'I don't really see it as that,' Hao says without hesitation. 'I do think that when people feel angry, if they have a forum to voice their anger, it helps the government build a more harmonious society, right? They shout. And then they calm down. They'll be better citizens. Blogging is just a continuation of that forum for voicing personal opinions.'

'So blogging won't overthrow the government?' I ask.

'I think when people talk about "democratising" China, it's going to be the outcome of so many forces,' says Hao. '*Everything* has to come together to push China to be more democratic. I don't think any single source can deliver the tool, or the hope, for China's democracy.'

Hao speaks with authority because he knows about the limits of freedom from personal experience. The day we met was one of the many grim, grey days at the beginning of the year, only months after his release from prison.

But he didn't want to be drawn on that at first, and so we talked about his early life. 'I think high school was the best part of my life,' Hao tells me. It was only a matter of years after the Cultural Revolution ended in 1976 that Deng Xiaoping started encouraging people to make money. 'But it was only in the mid-1980s that people felt totally free to try things,' says Hao.

In 1985, the China Export and Import Corporation bought four US films for release in China, including *Breakin'*, a breakdance film full of spandex and headbands. 'It was so exciting,' says Hao. 'It was a life-changing experience, to see all these Americans dancing to this music, the rhythm.'

At a time when wearing denim was still controversial, Hao and his friends, the bad boys at Chengdu Number 7 Middle School, added breakdancing to the school's end-of-year variety show. The word 'America' was planted in Hao's brain. By 1987, a handful of foreign exchange students were studying at Hao's school. 'We saw them on campus every day,' said Hao. 'They brought Madonna.' And soon there were books and tapes smuggled into China and copied amongst friends.

'We were so curious, so curious about anything from the outside. We'd talk about Freud. We'd talk about Einstein. We'd talk about Zen Buddhism.' Cultural Revolution became Cultural Renaissance.

The mood was catchy. An inspiring teacher encouraged Hao and his peers to think independently, a refreshing approach after the study-hard mantras of his childhood. Teacher Chen was a friend to her students. She was the Chinese 'Oh Captain! My Captain', with her own slogan. She declared repeatedly, 'You have only one life. Live differently!'

'She had a kind of an energy that had been suppressed for so long,' said Hao. 'But around us now there were a lot of debates, discussions, about democracy in China, about changing the constitution and striking out the communist rule. There was debate in the intellectual circles.'

But in the late 1980s, the ongoing process of opening up was still a fragile agreement brokered between the Chinese government and its people. 'We were like kids,' Hao said of his naivety. 'I think the whole country was, before the events of 1989.'

While shockwaves reverberated around the country (and the world) in June 1989, Hao was studying to get into an American graduate course. The 'open-door decade' had provided the opportunity for thousands of Chinese students to study abroad, including Deng Xiaoping's own son. In 1988, 68% of all Chinese students abroad were in the USA. By the time the Tiananmen Square protests broke out, more than 70,000 Chinese students and scholars had gone to America and, as a result of Deng's policies, not returned, according to the *New York Times*. In the aftermath of the Tiananmen protests tough new rules restricted immigration to America.

Hao suddenly had to choose whether to continue studying in China under new laws that required him to stay in Chinese employment for seven years, or to quit his degree before the regulations came into effect, and go to the land of breakdancing while he still could.

In 1992, aged 20, he accepted a scholarship to the University of Miami before transferring a year later to Brandeis University in Boston. It was the beginning of an extraordinary twelve years. He worked the dot-com boom in the Silicon Valley. He was given a green card and in 2002 he graduated from the University of Michigan with an MBA.

In America, Hao fell in love with the internet and when he returned to China in May 2004, he wanted to practise his writing and document his daily life. Beijing or Bust targeted two groups; two versions of himself. The first was the Chinese students overseas, for them 'to feel some kind of nostalgia, but to also feel happy about China's progress'. The second was the expats, who 'could totally see the ways I described Beijing, the details, the complexity and the bizarreness, some of the absurdity of living in Beijing'.

At first Hao's blog was not overtly political. He was more interested in contrasts, contradictions in the China changing before his eyes. Hao was like Beijing, himself on the brink of discovery. 'I chuckled at the thought that perhaps I'm just like this city,' he wrote, 'awkwardly exploring a new road with all the excitements and missteps.'

In China, borders are not lines on a map, but zones of contention, control and freedom, and the internet was more significant politically and culturally than any material frontier. The real lines of nation were being drawn in cyberspace.

Hao wanted his readers to see China as the confusing beast it was, cornered by centuries of misunderstanding and oppression, and skittishly coming out of the dark.

'What is China again?' he wrote. 'Perhaps I'm confused because I'm right in it.' Immersion, however, brought nuance. China, he argued, was a conceptual whole compiled from complicated and at times contradictory parts; over-engineered but iconic, like the Sydney Harbour Bridge.

Hao's trouble with the authorities started in mid-December 2005, through an invitation. He had been blogging about his thwarted attempts to film a documentary about Beijing's Christian churches, and was invited to spend Christmas with a well-known activist lawyer at one of the city's unofficial churches. China requires strict registration of all religious groups, and those that aren't registered attract police attention. The Jubilee Campaign, an inter-denominational lobby based in the USA, said in 2004 that about 300 Christians were in detention in China at any one time.

'I didn't want to get me or my family into trouble with the government,' Hao wrote on his blog. Nevertheless, he went to the church with a camera. He filmed the prayers and speeches and blogged the process, including a moment when he dreamed of 'heroically going to jail for doing the documentary'. He wondered aloud why the government would suppress these people's rights and concluded: 'Above ground or underground, the government can only promise 10% per cent GDP growth, while God promises a kingdom of heaven.'

Then the cops came. He describes the scene in a post on 16 January 2006. One policeman threatened to smash Hao's camera. 'I looked into his eyes and saw a trace of evil glinting over his rage,' he wrote. 'Not the evil of the communists, of the oppressors, or of Satan; but a hatred, out of deep frustrations, and a desire to destroy, both of which seem to have deep root in our culture.'

Hao handed over the tapes and – just over a month later – he disappeared.

The blog stopped. Then the news broke. An international online campaign was set up to lobby for his freedom. Hao got his own Wikipedia page. Reporters Without Borders campaigned via an open letter to Hu Jintao. Rebecca MacKinnon published an editorial piece in the *Washington Post*. The *Wall Street Journal* ran a feature about artistic freedom in China. His friends and family, denied access and representation, waited and waited.

Hao's distraught sister, Nina, blogged on Hao's behalf from Shanghai, detailing her own battles with the authorities for news of her detained brother. She began writing at the end of March after waiting five weeks for the authorities to release Hao. When they didn't, she went public.

Hao stayed locked away in solitary confinement for five months.

Back at Starbucks, a place designed as a black hole for cultural memory, we talk a lot about memory – Hao's and the nation's, and about the losses that change brings. He is openly compassionate about the generation who endured the Cultural Revolution. 'They really suffered a lot,' Hao tells me, 'and they haven't been able to tell their stories. And they suffer silently, either consciously, or subconsciously. But they cannot forget. And this China is moving so fast, it doesn't give the people a chance to reflect. And to me that's kind of sad.'

But while this older generation is possibly ignored, and certainly disenfranchised, Hao tells me that, like the rest of China, he wants to move on.

'Let's forget about this discussion about cultural heritage,' he says. 'Let's just be a curious nation. Because if the country's curious, you'll be able to go back into history and find what you like. You'll be able to learn from other cultures. You'll be a great nation.' This sounds reductive and sanguine from someone as intelligent as Hao, and I don't buy his throwaway optimism. I suspect he was wounded deeply in prison. He requests that I keep details of his imprisonment off the record. He still risks upsetting the authorities if he makes a wrong move.

I ask him to dig deeper. I ask him how this country can ever deal with loss.

'How do we as a nation be more reflective and, at the same time, be excited by the future? And how can we really work hard to address the problem *and* build a better future?' Hao asks back.

'Can you try to answer those questions?'

'I don't have the answers. I just see all these conflicts, the existence of decade-old grievances that haven't been addressed and also people's memories and sense of loss, as well as the future excitement. This contrast in China. I don't know how to address that.'

When Hao did at last come back to my computer screen, he returned to that coming-of-age period in Chengdu, the image of a Chinese boy breakdancing as his country starts to change.

'I'm not one of those who fight to break the shackles,' he wrote. 'But I can dance. Dance with my shackles. Dance with my bondage after the shackles. Dance to pray. Dance to hope.'

PART THREE
WINTER

CHAPTER 13

OLD BEIJING

I moved house in winter. November had brought the cold weather and by December the days were thin with light, the nights endless and bitter. The sky was matte mercury for weeks. The air was parched. It sucked at my skin, deeply creasing my hands.

I had three remaining goldfish. Jiaozi (dumpling) had already died. SoHo floated sideways in protest, and died soon after. My two plants, Pupsie and Wupsie, were sticks of their former selves.

On the evening I was to meet my guard for dinner, I arrived at the ornamental garden to see a stranger standing on his spot, rigid, and refusing to make eye contact. I returned every day at the same time for a week, but my guard had vanished without saying goodbye. I was sad. I didn't want to continue living alone.

'If you're unhappy, you should do something about it,' Jenny said, her arm linked in mine as we strolled up the Wangfujing shopping arcade. We had just seen *Harry Potter*. Our breaths steamed and mingled. 'There's no point in being unhappy, little pony head.' She smiled and threaded her fingers through mine. A room had become available near Houhai, with one of Jenny's friends, Yoni, a tall Californian consultant with big feet. I trusted Jenny, so I said yes.

I packed my strange collection of objects and, without emotion, switched off the lights and shut the big red doors of the courtyard house. I stopped by the auto-mechanic's workshop on Nanchizi.

My landlord wiped his hands with a greasy rag. He put his cigarette in his mouth and shook my hand with force, before returning to the undercarriage of a Mercedes.

I had craved the shufflings of others, of sitting in my boxers with a cup of tea talking about Tibet and Christmas and home with a flatmate. I missed spontaneous gatherings with friends for dinner, red wine. I wanted Sunday mornings and more tea with DVDs, popping into the neighbour's to borrow something, anything.

I also wanted a lesson in contrasts. The courtyard was quiet apart from the tinkering of bicycle repairmen. It had been salvaged from the wreckers and, like The Rocks in Sydney, made into a historical village, peaceful but removed, locked in stone, for us Westerners to walk on and live in. A storybook version of authentic Beijing. My new place, perched on the top floor of an apartment block, stared at other high-density apartments blocking out the sky. This was how the vast majority of Beijingers lived.

The erasure of old Beijing was most apparent in the area around my new apartment, between the Drum and Bell Towers and the Lama Temple.

Kinna, 22, a tour guide for the Beijing Hutong Culture Tour Company ('the only company that gives Hutong Tour with Government Approval') told me 6,000 families lived in the *hutong* webs around the towers. And about 60,000 people lived in the two square kilometres around the landmark, what's known as Shishahai (Ten Temple Lakes), making it one of the most densely populated areas in the city. These neighborhoods, this style of urban living, are unique to China and date back nearly 800 years. The word *hutong* comes from the Mongolian word *hottog* which means 'water well'. It's onomatopoeic; the sound a stone makes when dropped down a well and hits the water.

The two towers, the Drum and the Bell, stand at the northern tip of Beijing's traditional north-south axis. The Drum Tower, a commanding scarlet structure with multiple eaves, used to be the highest building in Beijing, and for centuries, writes historian Wu Hung, dictated the sleep patterns of millions of Chinese. Its drumming signalled the opening and closing of Beijing's nine ancient gates. After many fires, invasions and repairs since 1272 (when it was built by Kublai Khan), the Drum Tower has now become a major tourist attraction and still provides an impressive sweep of Beijing.

'Do you know what's going in there?' I asked Kinna from atop the tower, pointing to a hole of dirt, completely cleared.

'They think it will be a courtyard house museum,' said Kinna.

'They're clearing the courtyard houses to build a courtyard house museum?'

The irony was lost on Kinna. She doesn't care for the *hutong*. What was feared for her generation – a loss of tradition in the face of consumerism – is also the fear held for this area, as new buildings replace *hutongs*. It's a process that began in 1949, when the seat of government moved to the ancient city, a decision which Wu Hong calls the 'fatal moment in its survival'. After this, Beijing's urban face erupted in zits of redesign and construction.

Memories of the *hutong* and their values are fading fast among people Kinna's age. But she lived near the Bell Tower until she was eight, and remembers that until she was six her family shared her *si he yuan* (courtyard house) with other families.

'My favourite thing about living in the *hutong*,' she says, 'was coming home after school and playing with all the children in the streets. Because the streets were narrow and there were a lot of them, it was great fun.' She loved the community. Everyone knew everyone. She played *zhuo mi cang* (hide and seek) and *tiao fang zi* (hopscotch).

Kinna got her English name from one of her teachers at Beijing's expensive but well-regarded Wall Street Language School. She used family connections to get a job. Her cousin's wife worked as a Japanese tour guide in Beijing and introduced Kinna to the tour company, where she has now worked for six months. 'It's hard to find a job, so I'm very, very proud,' she says.

Kinna has since rejected the crowded, dilapidated courtyards. She now owns a four-door Peugeot hatchback that she drives into town from her parents' apartment on the East Fifth Ring Road. The new home is 100 square metres, smaller than a courtyard house, but she says, 'In Beijing, that's very big.' She has her own room there and her parents are soon to retire. She wouldn't live anywhere else.

Kinna is more interested in comfort and convenience. Given the grip of garbage on my shoes in the *hutong*, and the stench of the communal pit toilets, I don't blame her.

She takes me to visit Mr Wu, 74, who lives in a courtyard house on Jiao Jin Si Hutong. His house is 190 years old and wears its age well.

Mr Wu opened his house to tourists ten years ago, it's something to do since he retired. He gets paid by the tour company to show tourists Old Beijing. He is dressed in a green silk tunic and has gappy yellow teeth and smile lines around his eyes. 'Before, foreigners could only look outside and then they think they have seen Old Beijing,' he tells me. 'I think they prefer to see the inside.'

And inside is gorgeous, partly because the courtyard catches and holds the morning light. I feel insulated from the roaring city; it's silent and warm on this winter's day. Mr Wu's wife is reading a newspaper and eating biscuits in the sunny corner. She waves. A trellis bearing a grapevine runs above my head, and a pomegranate tree stands bare in the centre. The walls of the courtyard are made of grey brick and inset with red-framed windows on all sides. I look into rooms of aged furniture and photographs.

Mr Wu, a retired archaeologist, has lived here for over fifty years. He lives here now with his wife, a retired rubber-factory worker, his two sons, their wives, and his 13-year-old grand-daughter who is featured prominently in photos on the inside walls. The courtyard houses were designed for one family, but during the Cultural Revolution, many families crowded together, often dividing the courtyard into several living quarters.

Mr Wu has seen his city change more than many other septuagenarians elsewhere in the world and he's happy with what he sees.

We share green tea in the living area that contains a strange mix of modern appliances and antique sideboards. 'Beijing is bigger and more beautiful,' he says. 'The shops are more beautiful. Before, at six at night all the shops closed and turned off their lights. It was very dark. There was no one in the streets. Now, even at midnight, the centre of the city is very beautiful. All the lights are very beautiful. Before 1949 outside the Second Ring Road there were no buildings, just farms. Now there are so many tall buildings – and look at how many ring roads there are!'

But when he shakes my hand goodbye, I'm reminded that despite the famous Chinese saying *lao bu zou, xin bu lai* (if the old doesn't go, the new won't come), nostalgia provides a thick vein of emotion for people like Mr Wu who have lived through it all. He holds my hand for a moment longer and says slowly, like a teacher to a pupil, 'There's no Beijing without Old Beijing.'

Ich bin ein Beijing-er! Along with my new apartment, I have come into the possession of an ancient bicycle called Twaila, short for *tai kuai le*, meaning 'too fast'.

Twaila has no brakes and when we first went out she was snooty as hell about steering. Her handlebars continue to come loose whenever I need to do something important like, say, avoid cars.

Twaila's blue frame is pockmarked by rust but I don't mind. I admire Twaila more for her personality than her looks.

We're both awful in the mornings – she's a creaking mule of a thing and I'm ratty. But once we're rolling she scoots through traffic beating all manner of welded contraptions to the subway beneath the Lama Temple.

Here, Twaila says hello to a thatch of parked bikes and is looked after by a toothless mute man waving a red flag. I trust him. Separated, she joins her throng, I join mine.

On Twaila, Beijing makes sense. Riding a bike is the city's modus operandi and there are times when entire streets are taken over by bikes reaching critical mass.

When I pedal around the city a code is unlocked. Courtesies are offered up to us both – the nod of a head, eye contact, the tinkle of a bell. We are popular with children chasing after us in the alleyways shouting *lao wai, lao wai!* (foreigner, foreigner!).

The traffic makes more sense with Twaila too. There are around 10.2 million bikes in Beijing and two million cars. But some officials want the bikes to go. There is a push for all bikes in the capital to be taxed. Meanwhile, car numbers continue to soar – 1,500 are bought each day – adding to the chronic pollution.

But it's dangerous. There are no helmets (scary, when you see toddlers dinking with dads carelessly eating ice cream). Still, there's no doubt about a Beijing cyclist's skill. I've seen high-heeled grannies execute perfect dismounts and men moving fridges strapped to bikes through peak-hour traffic.

When I return from work, there's just Twaila and a dozen other bikes left at the stand. I pay the attendant two mao (about 1p). This is the time I like most, just me and Twyls hightailing it home through Beijing's wide avenues. I lock her up outside my apartment, say goodnight and head upstairs.

CHAPTER 14

GAY'JING

In the back corner of Le Petit Gourmand café in Beijing's embassy precinct, an air of secrecy hung between shelves heavy with French literature. I was there for an afternoon of gay politics.

'We should be quiet. We should be invisible,' Ming One whispered as I sat down. It was smoky. I imagined 1950s Paris. Winter jackets were heaped on a spare chair; coffee cups steamed. This was the weekly meeting of the Beijing Gay and Lesbian Alliance, on the third floor of a new building in Sanlitun. One of the café's managers was a friend of BGLAD and allowed the meetings as long as we bought enough hot chocolate. We were encouraged to look for new venues, however, as we ran the risk of getting too relaxed about the regular meeting spot.

BGLAD had 500 members and organised club nights and weekday discussion groups. It was run by an expat lesbian couple who also ran an event-organising business called Boa Productions. I had met Katie and Mikaela in mid-August during one of my first brushes with the gay scene at Destination, Beijing's busiest gay hangout. Katie told me then she wanted BGLAD to 'bridge the ideas of the West with the reality of China'. At first I thought this was paternalistic – do Beijing gays need the ideas of the West? – but I was curious. She signed me up to the mailing list. Over the following weeks I watched the alliance balloon with queer Chinese kids wanting to share their stories.

The strength of the alliance was tapping into this need to talk. It filled a gap. The agenda was wide-ranging and relevant: safe sex, dating, politics, film screenings, research, community activities. There was no topic that couldn't be hunted down, and open season was declared in the daily mailouts.

It felt like the salad days of an awakening gay movement. At the time, I wrote in my journal:

> There are hilarious similarities in gay cultures everywhere. One: the music. Two: the awkward solo approach to a bar under scrutiny. But there are lovely, curious differences too. No one is out. Everyone heads home early to see their mum. It's quite a touchy culture too, but not in a bad way. (Straight) Boys from the provinces hold hands walking down the streets, so physical intimacy is never a hurdle in Beijing. It translates to affectionate friendship for gay kids – there's always a hand on your knee. There's openness here. Some would think naivety. But I see a charting of new ground. Hunger. The word used for gay is *tongzhi,* which means comrade, or communist fighter; it was stolen after the Cultural Revolution and first used by Hong Kong queers. I like the appropriation of that word. It's the best I've heard. 'Gay' just meant happy before it was picked up in the West. *Tongzhi* has overtones of homoerotic militant solidarity! Showers and big boots; fighting a war of ideas.

But I didn't know the whole story.

Two days before the meeting at the French café, Chinese police had shut down the mainland's first-ever queer celebration, the Beijing Gay and Lesbian Culture Festival. I came to record their reaction.

Ming One is a skinny tour guide who speaks fast. Ming Two is a quiet, thoughtful translator. He takes time with words, they mean a lot to him. Coco, a student, was silent throughout the meeting.

There were only four of us. People had been too scared to turn up.

Ming Two kicked off the discussion quickly and got right to the point: Chinese society was a lie. Society looked stable, but once you scratched the surface of things, you fell headlong into the divide between public appearance and private desire.

'Chinese society is actually a very fractured society,' Ming Two said. He was angry about the shutdown. He saw it as an assertion of traditional Chinese values clamping down on difference. 'They won't allow anything unstable to break the balance of family, of normal relationships,' he said. The problem with the festival was that gay people had started to talk.

It might be years before pink really went with red. But at first glance, being gay in Beijing was OK. Bars like Destination were packed every weekend, even though they couldn't advertise. Gay kids were hooking up and starting relationships. At Destination, boys were kissing boys, girls were kissing girls. But the message was clear. Be gay. Have a dance. Fuck each other if you want. Just don't get political. Just don't talk about it.

'Don't ask. Don't talk. Don't question,' said Ming Two. 'Only then can you do what you like.'

Ming Two still had a foot inside the closet, but the day after the shutdown, he posted a comment to the BGLAD email list that read like a call to arms:

> I usually don't concern myself with politics. I can't even manage my own stuff! Now, I realise . . . the authorities just want to confine Chinese homosexual people to darkness and make their souls distort and suffer. They regard homosexuality as an 'unstable factor' which may, in their view, undermine what they call a 'harmonious society'. But it's unfair. This 'harmoniousness' is superficial. Should we sacrifice the minority's rights for the sake of fake stability? A real harmonious society can only be obtained by facing every problem squarely and doing our utmost to tackle them. I believe this

will change someday, but there is a long way to go. We need to keep trying.

The first-ever Beijing Gay and Lesbian Culture Festival had promised to be groundbreaking. The darlings of the growing movement were all on the door list for the opening cocktail party. Sun Zhongxin, the professor who started China's first queer-studies course at Shanghai's Fudan University in 2005 would host a curiously named panel discussion: 'Homo on Homo'. Li Yinhe, a celebrity academic from the Chinese Academy of Social Sciences would be giving the keynote address. Li authored *Their World*, which in 1992 was China's first academic attempt to describe the lives of gay men in China (it had a lot about cruising in public parks). She was also famous for submitting proposals to the government in 2003 and 2005 to legalise same-sex marriages. Both attempts failed, but she had credibility and she was all over hot-button issues like prostitution, marriage and HIV. Journalists had her number on speed-dial.

Panels to have been held were like gender-studies textbook titles: 'From Homosexual to Queer', 'Building Community Culture' and 'Representing Homosexuality'. Experts had flown in from the USA and Europe. The buzz around town was thrilling. Everyone was going to something over the three days of the festival.

The cultural festival was conceived in a climate of growing tolerance, or so it seemed. Even China Radio International had hopped on. The question 'Do you think there is enough knowledge about homosexuality in China?' was posed on *China Drive*. 'Is it still taboo? How much do you know about homosexuality?' Hundreds of responses flooded in and the reaction was a mixture of curiousity, misunderstanding and acceptance. Many listeners tried to explain the causes of homosexuality, and biology was the big winner.

'Frankly, I didn't like homosexuality,' wrote regular listener, Sand. 'But I've changed my mind since I read a book about the differences between men and women. Hormones are the real reason we're all different.' An anonymous contributor wrote: 'Growing up, someone could be shaped into abnormal behaviours for some reason. It can be called weird behaviour because it disobeys the laws of biology.' Potato Junior, a regular, had evidence at hand: 'Researchers in Sweden found that homosexual brains are different. So being gay is like being a left-hander, or a right-hander.'

And there were negative opinions. One listener believed that homosexuality turned arseholes 'rotten and black'. 'I'll bet they never taught that in Fudan University!' Someone called Vigor theorised that homosexuality could serve a communist purpose with the one-child policy, to keep a check on population. Homosexuality, to another, was the 'endmost expression of the pressure from life and work in a modern society'.

It was one of the most successful shows of the year. But it wasn't without its managerial hitches. Each morning, after I presented my on-air stock market rundown, the *China Drive* hosts would ask my opinion about the Topic of the Day. That day, I talked about *Brokeback Mountain*, the Ang Lee film, and said it was bizarre that it was banned when everyone I knew had seen it and could get it on the streets for 5 kuai (35p). I also said it was weird that the press celebrated Ang Lee – a Taiwan film director – as Chinese, while his film was banned on the Mainland. The programme manager Li Yun fired off a quick email to all *China Drive* producers: 'Please don't make any comments on government policies concerning politics and religion on our programme.'

I wrote back four minutes later: 'How can you talk about sexuality without talking about politics?'

We sallied back and forth: 'Dear, we can talk about sexuality without commenting on government policy on it,' she wrote, to which I replied, 'Sure. But the picture is incomplete then. If we can't tell the whole story – should we tell the story at all?'

Li Yun's final response was, 'It's challenging!'

The inaugural culture festival faced this same challenge. 'We are

Chinese gays and lesbians. We are here, and we want our rights,' festival organiser Xian told me. 'It's a statement that has a very political tone. How do you talk about being gay without being political?'

As it turned out, the authorities didn't think it was possible.

Festival organisers had booked a two-storey gallery in the fashionable 798 complex northeast of Beijing that could fit more than 500 people. On the Thursday before the opening night, police knocked on the organisers' door. They told Xian that a special permit was needed for an event with more than 500 people. Xian didn't believe them. 'Actually they didn't tell us the exact reason,' she said.

A new venue was needed and plans were made for On/Off, the first gay bar I went to in Beijing. Word went around that the festival was on the move. On/Off was a medium-sized bar done up with flashy lights, booths and tables, a catwalk, and a fleet of staff in matching outfits. The Long Island iced teas were brutal. It was more than rumoured to be full of 'money boys', male prostitutes who were often straight but came in from the provinces to set up a life in the capital. There had been a more official pimping system at Half and Half bar before it closed. Cute boy waiters were employed to keep the customers happy and were paid 500 kuai (about £40) a month. If one of the customers wanted to take them home, that was fine. The waiter had to leave 100 kuai (£8) at the bar, no matter what the customer was willing to pay for the night. At On/Off it was rumoured something similar was going on. Still, it was a fun place to dance to anthemic Kylie.

Xian thought the smaller venue was safer. 'It's a bar gathering! It's not the festival we planned but it's usually OK in a bar, there are so many parties in bars,' she said. It was around the end of the year, and Beijingers were staying warm with Christmas and end-of-2005 parties.

But police got wind of the move. Over thirty volunteers were preparing the venue, and by 5 p.m. there were over two hundred people outside waiting to join the party. Then two police vans pulled up, and volunteers were matched in number by officers who raided the bar.

They shut down the power and removed decorations, then closed the venue to review its licence. Xian said the police explained the bar was not fire-safe and that they didn't have the proper fire extinguishers. She laughed. 'Another excuse why we couldn't have the festival.'

The bar was shut down for three days – the entire length of the festival.

Wan Yanhai, an AIDS activist in Beijing, another of the festival's organisers and a man constantly in trouble with the police, was impressed by the crowd's response. 'My impression was that the audience, the organisers, were not threatened by the police. It was quite interesting. The police thought they were being very scary, but the people weren't scared.'

The next day, determined that something should go ahead, especially having dragged international scholars to town, the organisers booked a banquet hall opposite the Beijing Film Academy to host the speeches about gay identity. Finally, the gay community got to speak about itself.

CHAPTER 15
TONGZHI

Tongzhi – a word for both gay men and lesbians – literally meant 'comrade'. Someone with shared ideologies. It was a Chinese translation of the Soviet term, and Mao often used the word to address rallies. In 1989 a Hong Kong activist used the word to name the first gay and lesbian film festival in Hong Kong. *Tongzhi* spread quickly to Taiwan and then the Mainland. But while *tongzhi* described same-sex desire, it didn't exclude relationships with the opposite sex, getting married and living the Chinese hetero-dream of an apartment, babies and family get-togethers.

One boy I met – let's call him Pool Boy – was a *tongzhi*. He was a tall, 21-year-old actor with cheekbones you could stack books on and the sex drive of a three-balled frat boy. Pool Boy kept pictures of himself as the wallpaper on his mobile phone. I met him at Destination. He was wearing a sports headband, a tight t-shirt and jeans. He looked like Rain, the famous South Korean pop star, a poster of whom occupied a prominent position on my wall. Stephen had bought me the poster as a Christmas present.

Pool Boy had a girlfriend and he told me he loved women. But there was a lot of evidence suggesting that Pool Boy was gay, 100% gay. In the summer of 2006, we had a short and meaningless affair based entirely on his looks and my loneliness. For two weeks, Pool Boy's free days were spent tanning and reading fashion magazines on my veranda in a pair of blue Y-fronts. He wandered around the flat, cleaning and making iced tea before this all got too much and he retired for an afternoon nap.

Pool Boy's life was his dick – he talked about it all the time. In high school he was teased because his dick was too big. He told me he used to jack off (*da fei ji*: hit the aeroplane) with his flatmates all the time. If this isn't gay, I'm not sure what is, I thought.

He also told me he had sex with his girlfriend.

It was confusing. Not because I was falling for Pool Boy, or cared what he called himself (it was too fleeting, and he was too much of a narcissist, for that). I was confused because he wanted to set me up with one of his female classmates.

I confronted him one night at Kai bar. 'So what's the deal, are you gay?'

'Sleeping with guys is private,' he said, 'and I can't tell anyone about it. I will never get a job.' Pool Boy had two years left of acting school.

'What about your girlfriend? What will she think if you get married and you still want to sleep with guys?'

'I won't do that when I'm married,' he said.

'Why not?'

'Cos I will love my wife.'

And so my days of having a Chinese manservant came to an astonishingly quick end, never to be repeated. I think I had served my purpose for Pool Boy, though – lust, uncomplicated by the future. Exactly the kind of denial I was in the market for.

And then it hit me – my culture made my sexuality the biggest thing about me. Pool Boy's culture didn't have a direct translation for the English word 'sexuality'. Until the 1990s, his culture had never treated sex or sexuality as something that could exist outside the highly structured system of family. Hong Kong activist Chou Wah-Shan argues that before the 1990s, 'the majority of Mainland Chinese were basically unaware and unconcerned about the issue of homo/bisexuality and sexual orientation in general'.

Pool Boy felt uncomfortable with my divisions of gay and straight.

Did living as a gay man mean he couldn't get married? Did it mean he had to love and have sex with one person, a man, his whole life? And what about his parents? Did it mean that he wouldn't fulfil his role for them in being married and having children?

Chou Wah-Shan writes that by exhorting Chinese *tongzhi* to come out, there's a risk of making them non-beings in Chinese culture. Becoming 'gay' or 'lesbian' made sexuality more important than having a family, and that was too high a price to pay. Pool Boy might even cease to exist.

Was Pool Boy bisexual? Maybe, if he'd grown up in Australia. But here he was *tongzhi*. The word also embraces what we in the West blandly call 'gay friendly' too, the fag-hags, fag-stags, political sympathisers, drag queens and kings and those of us simply living outside the genders. But it isn't a political attempt to include everyone like the word 'queer' does.

The English word 'gay' tends to lump everyone together, perhaps because we can live relatively uncomplicated gay lives. 'Gay' has also won us a bunch of battles; it's a banner under which we can unite and fight. *Tongzhi*, instead, encompasses the many differences between people. *Tongzhi* means that at some point – maybe on weekends, maybe in park toilets, maybe when I talk to my friends, maybe when I'm getting a guy off – we share this one desire. You might see *tongzhi* blowing each other in the bathrooms of Destination. But ask the same guys whether they love and cherish their girlfriends and they'll answer yes, absolutely-why-would-you-even-ask, yes.

My cultural bias at the time thought that Pool Boy couldn't see the contradictions in the way he lived because he was a bit dumb (he *was* a bit dumb), or worse, not brave enough. But in the end, Pool Boy had never thought about it, and my obsession with a homo-hetero divide didn't make sense to a boy fucking both genders without any complaints from either. I went travelling and received messages telling me he missed me. But I doubted it. He seemed pretty OK.

Tongzhi weren't all Pool Boys. Some had come out to their families and rejected marriage. I met these *tongzhi* as regularly as I met the Pool Boys of Beijing. Ming Two was one of these.

I caught up with him again in the French café in Sanlitun. I asked him about the differences between gay and *tongzhi*. 'What I was struggling with was not whether I was gay,' he said. 'It was about whether I could be compatible with my surroundings. It's not about my identity. It was about how to be adaptable.'

Identity versus adaptability. *Tongzhi* allowed Ming to be adaptable in a way that 'gay' did not. 'Gay' fused politics and sex, but according to Chinese reality, *tongzhi* provided the option to live these lives separately.

Ming Two knew the word 'gay'; he liked it, used it, and wanted to fight for it, despite the complications presented by Chinese culture. He was insatiably curious about the gay scene in Western countries. For him, the West was a fantasia of parades and same-sex marriage. It was freedom.

Ming Two said that China had come a long way. 'The situation in recent years is changing for the better,' he conceded. 'On TV, shows have started to talk about being gay. It will change with time, step by step. Compared with ten years ago, the situation is totally different.'

In 1997 the law most affecting *tongzhi*, article 160 in China's 1980 criminal code, was dropped. Officially known as the 'hooliganism' law, it was a catch-all, and enforcement was inconsistent. But in day-to-day policing, the law was used to net gay men cruising parks and toilets for sex. This scenario was depicted in *East Palace, West Palace* (*Dong Gong, Xi Gong*), the mainland's first gay film, made in 1996.

A decade later, people are more tolerant, said Ming. 'But we're talking another ten years. Well, maybe not even then. In ten years, the Communist Party'll still govern us and they'll never let gay culture be mainstream. But for our private lives, it will be more like in Hong Kong or Taiwan.'

While the Aibai Culture and Education Centre's 'FAQs for Gays

and Lesbians' makes it clear that homosexual sex is legal, there
are still gay arrests. In May 2006, Mr X was arrested in Beijing
and sentenced to a year in prison. Under his internet screen name
'Beijing Sky', he had been organising 'Beijing Cool Guys Passion-
ate Friendship Parties' since March 2005. Organising sex between
three or more people in any venue was a criminal act. Individuals
could be penalised a maximum fine of 200 kuai (£16). If the situation was deemed more severe, individuals could be detained for five
to ten days and fined a maximum of 500 kuai. By June 2005, Mr
X's sex parties were packed and business was booming. He charged
up to 50 kuai on the door, and produced CDs, and 'other objects for
services'. On 11 November 2005 the police received a tip-off. They
arrested Mr X and found ten men, aged 29 to 34.

Having sex in parks was also breaking the law, if you could stomach it at all. Cruising isn't known for its salubriousness and one
account of Dongdan park in Beijing by Chinese-Singaporean blogger Yawning Bread makes that clear:

> Chinese public toilets, as many of us know, plumb remark-
> able depths of quality . . . [this one] had a row of broken or
> leaky urinals, but obviously, nobody relied on them anymore.
> Instead, the janitor hung paint cans from the faucets that
> once used to flush their respective urinals. It was apparent to
> all that one shouldn't pee into the urinals, but into the paint
> cans, and when a can got full to the brim from accumulated
> pee . . . the janitor would come in and haul the can out.
>
> Behind the paint-can guard of honour, there were more
> exhibitionists in the squat cubicles, doorless, in fine Chinese
> tradition. I noticed a guy squatting in one, wanking furiously.

After our interview, I made my usual offer to Ming: 'I've asked all
the questions so far. Do you have any questions for me?'

'Yes, I do', Ming said. 'Have you ever used – what do you call
them? Glory holes?'

My sip of coffee became a gulp.

'I mean, how do you know how to find one?' he asked.

'A *glory hole*?' Maybe Ming meant something else.

'Are they everywhere in America? Or are they just in the back rooms of gay bars? Do people have sex in back rooms of gay bars, because there are no back rooms in gay bars in China.' Yep, Ming meant glory hole.

'Where did you learn about them?' I asked.

'I saw pictures online. They could never be in public toilets, right? Because straight people would wonder why there's a hole. It could all go wrong. How does it work? They must only be in the back rooms of gay bars,' Ming reasoned.

Unfortunately I was ignorant of glory-hole etiquette. Apparently you had to tap your fingers in the hole, or beckon. I told Ming this. He nodded. That made sense.

I was delighted that Ming thought sticking your dick through a wall for anonymous sucking was the height of Western sexual freedom. 'I guess people just know about the glory holes from rumour, or their friends, and they go to see for themselves,' I said.

We chatted about going to gay bars and dating for another half hour. Had I ever had a one-night stand? Did I like one-night stands? How do you deal with the morning after a one-night stand? What happens when you see the one-night stand again in public? When you like someone a lot, what does sex mean? At what point in the relationship was it OK to have sex? Was I afraid that I might be too horny and forget to use condoms? Did I know anyone who had HIV? Is there a difference between hugging and sex? I ordered another coffee and began answering his questions as best I could.

Ming was born in Sanming, a newly industrialised city in Fujian. Fujian was the province from which most people fled across the strait to Taiwan after the PRC was declared in 1949. In 2005, the city became famous for harbouring the third human death from the bird flu. In 1988, the State Council chose Sanming to experiment with new forest management. Reforestation began, and resources for the first time were owned by village committees through distribution of stocks and managed under contracts.

Sanming, like the rest of Fujian, flourished from the influx of foreign investment in manufacturing in the 1990s. Foreign enterprise enjoyed preferential tax breaks, use of the land and raw materials. It was here that Ming spent the first eighteen years of his life in a small apartment allocated by the government.

Ming, like others of his generation, took notice of Western ideas. He says that without *The Wedding Banquet*, Ang Lee's 1993 film, he would never have learned the word 'gay'. The film itself is about the tensions between a gay Western lifestyle and the traditional Chinese values of filial responsibility. 'I read some books and also watched some movies. And then I came to think about it. I accepted that I was gay very quickly.' He had some crushes on girls: the popular or brainy girls. But he never dated them.

Ming is fascinated that I live an 'out' life, like in the movies. He envies that my parents know. He wants to tell his parents, but is scared to. 'My parents are very traditional. So it's hard for them to accept new things. They would be shocked. And they wouldn't be able to sleep. It would be too much for them. And the best way is to hide this from them.'

After I told people I was gay – after I said the words – I thought the world would spin anew with nights of uninterrupted sleep. I'd have an appetite and I'd work out. I would pass to the other side, to a land of sexual careerists.

Instead I stooped in the shower – crying – and stared at the tiny squares of tiling. 'Gay' didn't liberate. It hurt me and it hurt others. It consigned me a size and a shape and shore off the edges of my other identities. I knew I would repeat this coming out a thousand times. I was linked through this word to all my future selves like stretched out, concertinaed men cut from paper. There I was, from here until the end of time, repeating gay, gay, gay, gay.

In this, Ming and I shared something. A relationship with words that relieved the pressure with pleasure. For adaptability. To fly, when the world wants to pin you to the corkboard for display.

When Ming started working in 2001, the year China struck homosexuality off the mental illness list, the internet was booming. In that year, there were nearly a million registered internet users in Ming's home province alone. 'I didn't know how gay people had sex,' he said. 'I really didn't know the ways they had sex. I was taught by porn.' He was surprised by some things he saw, and intrigued by others. But he was turned on and he saw a possible sexual future for himself. The internet, and the safety it provided gay people, was Ming's springboard for diving in to the deep end.

It still took a few years before Ming had sex for the first time. He was 26 years old.

'It was in a park,' he said with a smile. At the time he was working in Xiamen, a commercial hub on the coast of Fujian. Ming cruised the park and came across an ordinary, middle-aged man. 'And then he took me home.'

CHAPTER 16

LALA

The word *lala*, to describe lesbians, was derived from a 1994 book called *Eyu Shouji* (*The Crocodile's Journal*), by Taiwanese author Qiu Miaojin. Qiu, at 25, was already a starlet in Taiwan's literary avant garde. Two major awards for short fiction catapulted her into the glare of the media spotlight, which at the time was obsessed with the rise of gay culture. Lesbianism had all the right ingredients for the sensationalist press, and Qiu was the natural poster girl.

The Crocodile's Journal won the *China Times* Honorary Prize for Literature in 1995. It's a surreal trip around contemporary Taipei through the eyes of Lazi, a humanities student at National Taiwan University. Lazi's story is a satirical take on the emotional turmoil of being a lesbian college student, writes scholar Tze-Ian D. Song. The book is based on Qiu's own experiences of painful same-sex love affairs. Lazi wakes up in her room at midnight and reads the idols of the modish, self-aware elite: Dazai Osamu, the profoundly pessimistic Japanese writer obsessed with suicide, and Kierkegaard.

Lazi's narrative is combined with Kafkaesque sections about a childish crocodile living in Taipei. 'Crocodile' must wear a tight-fitting human suit to pass in society. A media circus reports that crocodiles are running rampant on the island, and TV viewers become fanatical about trying to detect real crocodiles in public. But the shy 'Crocodile' longs to say hello, and sends a TV station a home video in which she takes off her human suit to reveal her true form. She looks like everyone else. Just a little greenish.

'Crocodile' and the name Lazi were adopted as code for 'lesbian' in lesbian magazines and chat rooms throughout the 1990s, but the reasons for this are complicated. The first reason is a pun. Lazi resembles the beginning of the English word 'lesbian' when said with a heavy, camp American drawl. *Laaahsbian*. The name Lazi itself has a tricky literal translation into English, something like 'recruiter'. La is the Chinese character meaning 'pull'. You see it on doors everywhere. 'Zi' makes the verb into a person. Lazi became a lesbian hero in the underground gay scene of Taiwan, and *lala* caught on in a big way. When the Mainland got wired into the internet in the late 1990s, the word leapt into real-life communities.

Sadly, Qiu killed herself in Paris where she was studying psychoanalysis a year after her book was published. She plunged a knife into her heart and died instantly. No one knows why. Just before she died, she wrote another Taiwanese *lala* classic called *Mengmate Yishu*, Montmartre Testament.

'Taipei's literary scene is smallish,' says Fran Martin, an expert in Taiwanese queer fiction at the University of Melbourne. 'Qiu's youth, major talent, controversial subject matter, and sensational death made her a prominent figure. Also, for the nascent lesbian communities and individuals her books were immensely significant, for many people the first representation they saw in Chinese, and set in places they knew, of female same-sex desire and romance.'

Today, *lala* is quite a common term. But it is still hard to say what it actually describes. It is less about an identity, I think, than 'lesbian'. Many *lalas* I met dated boys, had sex with boys, but identified as *lala*. They fell in love with women, or wanted to be with women, or even wanted to conform to a gender stereotype that was different from the strict rules of Chinese femininity. *Lala* was perhaps more about what you did, rather than simply a name. It was an attitude, a stance, rather than something describing whom you slept with. It allowed conversation to happen around the issues of desire and attraction in a very Chinese context where marriage – and the relationship with a husband – was still an expectation for most women.

'So how many girlfriends have you had?' I ask Anna, a slight and pretty girl with flowers in her hair. She is wearing hot pink lipstick, and sits restless opposite me in the green and brown vinyl booth.

'Just two,' she giggles.

'How long did you see them?'

'One of them was just for one week. The other . . . ' She pauses and wiggles in her seat.

'Have you heard of 419?' the stockier girl sitting next to Anna grins. Anna blushes. 'Four One Nine. It sounds like "for one night". It's what we call a one-night stand,' says the girl. Her name is Yong Mei.

'Yeah. OK. All right,' Anna pipes up. 'It was a 419. But really, I think emotion is very important for me. If I have the emotion for somebody, then I will also have the sexual feelings. No emotion, no feeling. And beauty! I love beauty. So I am single.' She lowers her face and shoots a glance at Yong Mei. 'Besides, I think most *lala* aren't very beautiful.'

Yong Mei rolls her eyes at Anna like she's a silly girl. Yong Mei is a *T*, a tomboy, butch. Anna is a *P*, short for *po*, which means wife. I've seen this disconnect before.

'So are *lala* bars for picking up, or what?' I ask.

'No no. They're just normal bars for making friends,' says Yong Mei. 'This is a place where we can communicate. You can talk and make new friends here.'

'Do you think a lot of *lala* are afraid to come out to places like this?'

'A lot. Most lesbians,' says Yong Mei.

'Me!' cries Anna and squeezes her eyes tight. 'It's a secret. My family is very traditional and wouldn't accept it.'

'Do you have a boyfriend at the moment?'

'Nah, right now I don't. I used to have lots of boyfriends, you know. No, not lots. Just some.'

Yong Mei looks at Anna bemused. This is Yong Mei's fifth *lala* salon. The salon is every Saturday afternoon, except during Spring Festival. It started two years ago.

'Sometimes it's good just to sit here, because it's free and you can talk about whatever you want,' she says.

Next to the monolithic Ministry of Foreign Affairs there's an unpopulated strip mall. Inside, at the top, a small restaurant serves an unlikely concoction of fried American food. There are oil paintings of Sinatra and Springsteen and a fake bull's head fastened to the wall. The brightly lit booths are greasy to the touch and glow orange under the words *Le Jazz* written with a long tube of fluorescent light.

The TVs are belting out Taiwanese pop, and just beneath that sound is the twang of forty women chatting earnestly in Mandarin. Most of the women are in their early 20s. 'At the Maple Bar, the longest-running lesbian bar in the whole of China,' my host Xian tells me, 'the average age is probably early 20s, or just 20.' But the clock is ticking even for these young *lala*, says Xian. 'People come to our salon and say they are worried about the future. What if you are 25 and your parents start to ask "Right, do you have a boyfriend? When are you going to get married?"'

Marriage is today's topic and debate hums in the booths.

'Society thinks gay people don't have true love, and that every gay couple is just playing around and goofing off,' argues Yong Mei, 24. 'It's such a traditional Chinese concept that people who are in love with each other should get married. It is not about kids or other stuff like that. It's about love. Since gays can't marry in China, people think gay relationships are unacceptable.'

'My parents would like me to marry some man,' says Anna with sad eyes.

'Will you get married?' I ask Yong Mei.

'Yeah. I'll marry if it becomes legal for gays. If someday I wanted to marry a man, my parents would think I was crazy. They know I'm a *lala*. My parents are supportive of me being a lesbian.'

'They know?' Anna's face is aghast.

'Of course they know,' Yong Mei dismisses her.

'Oh wonderful, wonderful.' Anna bows her head deferentially. 'You're very lucky.' Her bowing turns cheeky and Yong Mei turns away from her.

Yong Mei didn't grow up here. She dropped out of college and ran to Beijing with a broken heart. No one will pay Yong Mei to do research in her beloved area of sociology because she doesn't have a degree, but she's making some ends meet with freelance writing. 'I have to stay in Beijing,' she says, 'because I want to find the representatives who attend the government's meetings and persuade them to help me push gay marriage legislation.' Yong Mei works closely with sexologist Li Yinhe on political strategies and runs a blog dedicated to getting the marriage proposal passed.

Yong Mei's hometown of Tacheng is a rural centre of 50,000 on the windswept border of China and Kazakhstan, at the edge of China's vast ethnic Xinjiang province. Her father is a labourer, and her mother sells *xiaðian*, traditional Chinese innersoles, on the street. Yong Mei is of Miao nationality, one of fifty-five ethnic minorities recognised by the Chinese government. There are only 8,000 Miao in the upper reaches of Xinjiang, an area famous for devastating snowstorms that kill hundreds every few years. The blizzards have nothing on Beijing, which still blows Yong Mei's mind. It's dirty, exciting and cosmopolitan.

'People don't know each other here,' she says. 'Lots of people are like me, not local, so there are no parents here. We don't have to worry so much about being found out. I can walk with my girlfriend on the street.'

In Xinjiang, her failed crush on her college engineering teacher left her ostracised and heartbroken. 'When she found out that I was in love with her, she never spoke to me again.' Lovesick, humiliated, she ran away. Here in the city, she has begun the first scary steps of a real relationship. 'I always wished I could have a girlfriend. I never knew what it would be like. I just followed the feeling.' She has been going out with her girlfriend for 138 days.

Small towns breed small minds, says Yong Mei. Her parents reacted badly when she came out. Coming out at Spring Festival is like coming out at Christmas: the family drama to end all family dramas. Yong Mei ruined the week, and the family fell apart that year. 'My parents were crying, angry, depressed. They said it was the end of the world. They said that if I told other people they would kill themselves.' Things are better now. No one talks about it. But it's better, just better.

Our café booth swells with *lala*. I assemble fragments of conversation into a current of girl-chat – Who's your new girlfriend? Oh her. Didn't she go out with whatshername? The basketballer? I like those shoes. I think that girl is cute, but she never says hello. What's her deal? Her hair is cute, but it's such a lesbian haircut. She has a lesbian name too. I heard she was studying acting. Has she been on TV? Yeah, that new girl you're seeing. The basketballer. My girlfriend, oh man, I don't understand her at all. All I know is that she weirds me out. And I'm like, can we just have sex? Then, she started snoring, in my house. Snoring.

As more girls join us, Anna points out the *T*s and *P*s, not that I need much help, the categories are well maintained. There are also *Pure T*s, *Iron T*s, *Hard T*s, *Baby T*s. The list is endless.

'I'm a *Pretty T*,' Anna says proudly, and shows the circle her face. This means she's butch deep down but just looks feminine. Everyone objects.

'You are not!' says Amy, sitting next to Anna, and hits her on the arm. 'You are a *P*! A *P*!'

Two *T*s join us, Gogo and Sam. They edit China's first and only lesbian magazine, *Les+*. The name of the mag is a pun: the Chinese plus sign is *jia*, which sounds like 'family'. It's a handsome, matte-printed black-and-white zine with a pink spot-colour and contains photos of the lesbian scene, advice, gossip and girls galore. Two thousand copies are printed every month. It's free in bars and at the salon, and it's available on the web for 3 kuai (25p).

We leaf through the pages. It contains everything a *lala* could need. The biography of a lesbian couple's cat. Common reasons for vaginal bleeding during intercourse and some practical and common information on the hymen. There's also an instructive picture of an orchid with the names of various parts of the vagina applied to the flower. An introduction to Marxism and Feminism follows. Is spermless conception a technological possibility? What's the legal deal with gay marriage?

'Most lesbians are underground,' says Gogo, 'and they feel depressed and lonely. But I think we – this lesbian community right here in Beijing —' she looks around the table for confirmation, 'we're really happy. So I want more lesbians to know about us. I want them to be happier and more confident.'

'Last year our mag was just a thin paper, but look at it now!' says Sam.

She turns to me. 'Articles in the media always say that lesbians' lives are miserable. Our aim is to change this misunderstanding.'

'Low on demands, high on emotions,' my translator Elena proclaimed later. Elena grew up in Taiwan but now lives in New York. 'The personal narratives are noxiously sappy, and it's filled with cheesy stories about love and romance. It's sort of like reading people's diaries, not very exciting diaries.'

Elena grew up with propaganda speeches in China and *Les+*'s writing style makes her suspicious: 'All so glory-filled and grandiose-toned, there is an exaggeratedness to their language that I find artificial and contrived. None of those stories ever mention sex. No enjoyment of sex, no good sex, bad sex, nothing. The main themes for the *Les+* crowd are the searches for love and romance, marriage and babies.'

Elena seems to be right. Just as in male *tongzhi* communities, family comes first for *lala*. Much of the magazine is devoted to a pregnancy diary written by a lesbian couple.

Sam and Gogo will keep publishing. 'There are more and more people like us who are willing to come out. Public opinion and the government's attitudes are getting better,' says Sam.

'If you want to make your own life happy and be accepted by society, you have to fight together with the whole lesbian community to change lesbian life for everybody.'

With two hours of talk still to go, I nod at Xian and peck Anna on the cheek. I shake Yong Mei's hand and slip out down the escalators leaving the salon patter for the adolescent grunt of the street.

CHAPTER 17

APARTMENT 1601

I rarely leave the familiar confines of the Second Ring Road. The city locked inside it remains pretty stable, but outside the road, and off the edge of my Beijing map, are the demons and dragons of mass construction. It takes forever to get anywhere out here: cars roar like pack animals straining against the city, trolley-buses spark on wires. Commuters stare blankly for hours, like Charon's cargo.

I have my final appointment with two gay activists in a bedroom on the sixteenth floor of a building in Beijing's north, eight kilometres from the centre.

Their apartment is in Building 20 of over thirty drab high-rises near the cut of the North Fourth Ring Road. Numbers and major intersections are used to navigate this Beijing, not names. These numbers are displayed on ubiquitous metal plates. So I count out twenty buildings, sixteen floors, four apartments, and ring the doorbell of 1601.

The view from the sixteenth floor shows a city rippling with construction. The pale sun sets low across Yayuncun, the site of the 1990 Asian Games that galvanised Beijing towards its 2008 bid.

Yayuncun will become the new Beijing Olympic Green, the environmentally sustainable centrepiece of Beijing's bid. It will crown the city's north-south axis that passes through the Forbidden City and Tiananmen Square. The park will become the capital's largest public space, a staggering 1,135 hectares. Imagine ripping up about half of Sydney's CBD. Sixty per cent of that will be forest.

The Olympic Green will contain the International Broadcast and Television Centre, the National Aquatic Centre and the National Stadium. The Urban Planning and Design Institute of Tsinghua University has promised to give Beijing an 'urban green lung', with water recycling, integrated use of green power, and even a system installed to give 'intelligent early warning of thunder and lightning'.

North of the Olympic Green, above the Fifth Ring Road, there will be a sanctuary for animals and for the recovery of flora. The park will even continue across a bridge spanning the road to prevent wildlife from becoming roadkill.

I see the lattice beams of the new National Stadium poking up like the bare twigs of a bird's nest. The area is covered with cranes and dust, like dragons' heads dancing in the fumes of a New Year parade. Yellow construction hats march two-by-two along the road.

And while thirty-three million trees have been planted across the city to grow before the Olympics, this area now is still far from green. It's brown. And the lungs struggle for air.

Millions of people live in this area of Chaoyang, Beijing's largest district that shoehorns the entire north and east of the city. From up here, the bleak urban magnitude of Beijing is dizzying. Compounds are cut off by the big multi-lane roads, cordoned off into mini-metropolises behind high concrete walls. There is limited access to streets. The Chinese 'courtyard' tradition that contains everything within four walls has been super-sized by modern development. The result is isolation and anonymity. *One size fits most.*

Perhaps the Olympic Green will deconstruct the city's north. But for now, Beijing is *programmed*. It's like living in a 1990s computer game before the graphics got good: boxy and monochromatic. The engineers, like Beijing's urban planners, coded one of everything then repeated. The windows, the doors, the layouts, the floor spaces, the lifts, the air-conditioning units and often the front-door codes are all the same. 'I've been here before', I think, standing in a concrete foyer, a dark hallway, damp floors with no carpet.

A gay couple and a lesbian couple share Apartment 1601 with two very noisy cats. In the third bedroom is China's largest research and resource centre for gay and lesbian issues. This amounts to a floor-to-ceiling bookshelf lining one wall, stuffed with vertical files of paper, pamphlets, books and other reading material. Under the tables, and stuffed into corners, are cardboard boxes filled with books, magazines, information. I wonder if the authorities know this is here. And I wonder again about the energy required to run an entire movement from a converted bedroom.

The nine-month-old cat Fa Ching gnaws at one of the boxes and then curls up in my lap. I call it 'pooch', it's the size of a dog. There's one PC and a laptop on the cluttered table.

In January 2005, Xian started a community-action group called Common Language. She says her aim is to help 'community empowerment by information'. The group's main activity is the *lala* salon. Common Language also staffs a hotline for lesbian and bisexual women every Wednesday and Thursday.

Xian, 34, and Binglan share a vision for the gay movement in China. They found a rental, since neither had enough money to support their own offices. They now work closely together on a range of projects, like flying kites off the Great Wall to celebrate International Pride Month. 'Both of us think it's important for gays and lesbians to celebrate their identities in public,' says Xian. Binglan makes me tea in a decorative green pot. In 1998, he started China's most popular gay website. Aibai.cn gets one hit every four seconds inside China and it still contains its original mix of news, literature, gossip and gay-rights news from around the world. The only point of law governing gay content on the web concerns 'the dissemination of obscenity, pornography and other undesirable information', and this is mainly to do with violence and abuse. Everything else is open slather on aibai.cn, including personals.

The website is staffed by volunteers from around the country; it costs only $125 per month to maintain, whereas *Les+* costs around $1,000 to print each issue. The internet is not only affordable, sometimes it's the only way to do activist work.

Outside the windows of Apartment 1601, night is setting in. The traffic doesn't stop, and the pollution will worsen as daytime restrictions on factories and large trucks lift for the night. Tests show that midnight is the most polluted time in Beijing, especially beyond the Fourth Ring Road where 200 steelworks and factories have relocated in an attempt to cleanse the city. The three metres of sulphur is now lit from below, like we're hovering above Hades.

'What do *tongzhi* want, what concerns them?' I ask the activists.

'*Tongzhi* in China,' says Binglan, 'just want a better life.'

'Doesn't everyone?'

'A lot of gays and lesbians *do* think about rights,' Binglan clarifies, 'but they don't relate them to *human rights*. They only talk about the right to love, the right to marry. It's more about the rights that relate to their everyday lives. They don't really call them rights.'

'So what are the activists fighting for?' I ask.

'We do a lot of grassroots work,' says Xian, stroking Fa Ching who has now crawled into her lap, a great ball of white hair. 'It's about empowering the group. And then we try to have the younger ones come out. In the end maybe this will change things.'

'So that each individual can know the rights he has,' Binglan concludes, 'and be brave enough to go for his rights. I think that's the goal for everyone. Gay rights are key to establishing democracy in China.'

CHAPTER 18

THE WHORE
OF THE ORIENT

Sydneysiders are snobs about fireworks. We pour millions into New Year displays over the harbour then smugly watch lesser celebrations domino around time zones: the solemn ringing of a town bell; the frigid Northern Hemisphere winter.

But this Sydneysider has to concede: other cities know how to party. Beijingers stockpiled fireworks for weeks leading up to the lunar New Year's Eve that kicked off the annual Spring Festival at the end of January. (Spring Festival in the chill of winter. Go figure.)

China was expected to unleash 1 billion kuai (£82 million) worth of fireworks and firecrackers over the 2006 Spring Festival period, as more than 200 cities joined the capital to blow stuff up, despite healthcare groups raising concern about injuries.

The government had lifted a pyrotechnics ban and you could feel twelve years of repressed ignition inching across the city. The air crackled with it. There was hysteria as premature rockets hit the sky ahead of schedule, like sports cars jockeying for pole position.

At midnight, Stephen and I watched the city rock like a war zone. The most expensive crackers shot high in the sky and exploded in magnificent colours. The largest I saw was a pine-green plume over a footbridge outside the Workers' Stadium. Most, however, were cheaper low-range crackers, white and fizzy and without the clout to reach above the rooftops, and the noise ricocheted around the city. Explosions erupted on every corner; it was deafening, and as bright as daylight. From above, the city must have surged with light for several minutes.

We thought we might go deaf after one rocket sprayed shop-fronts and rooftops around the Houhai lakes. While we scampered for cover, locals applauded. Gleeful old men continued till dawn lighting cherry bombs and Roman candles, recalling simpler times when a traditional cracker and a dumpling meant a party. Alongside the old men were the middle-aged, lighting firework after firework, often with cigarettes. One bang was never enough.

One Western friend commented that this is what happens when you deny self-expression for decades. A bang to scare away a ghost becomes an opportunity for insurrection.

Spring Festival, like everything else in China, was changing. It had become the largest human stampede in the planet's history. A population seven times the size of Australia's travelled back to their hometowns by train. The Ministry of Railways said that five million more Chinese travelled by train in the lead-up to the Spring Festival than the previous year. The ministry added 6,620 additional services to the rail network to cope.

So long and arduous was the trip that some people resorted to wearing nappies. Reuters reported that sales of adult diapers in China's southern city of Foshan soared 50% in the lead-up, with train commuters preferring to shit themselves rather than battle carriage-loads of passengers to get to the toilet.

If you had been squeezed into an overnight standing-room carriage on a Chinese train you wouldn't baulk at the idea. It would be small discomfort compared to the myriad sights and stench: cigarette smoke and ash, children pissing on the floor, and the endless chowing down on shrink-wrapped chicken's feet.

As a sign of the times, mobile phones coordinated the exodus. China's 400 million or so mobile phone users (a number increasing at a rate of three to five million per month) sent twelve billion SMS messages over this period. That's a lot of sore thumbs. That's thirty messages per person.

I was reminded of Christmas. The same tacky sparkly decorations, the same materialism. Instead of Santa Claus, the traditional figures of a small boy and girl lighting crackers adorned everything from KFC meals to Coke bottles. McDonald's, for example, was giving out *hong bao* (money-filled red envelopes) with a burger, redeemable for a soft-serve.

Despite thirty-six people being killed in a fireworks factory explosion on New Year's Eve, and the thirty-five tonnes of firework-debris, ash and tickertape on Beijing streets (with 20,000 cleaners to clean up) the fireworks were here to stay as one concession to the good ol' days.

The noisy festive season led to many sleepless nights. On the sixth floor of our apartment block, crackers exploded at window height. I was tense and tired. I needed to get out of Beijing. I booked a ticket to Shanghai – the Whore of the Orient, the Paris of the East – and got on a plane the next day.

I burst into spontaneous laughter at the sheer speed of the train that pulled me into the city from the airport. I felt cleansed by this rainy Shanghai. I liked the sounds of cars on wet roads. I watched real rain clouds swirl around the impossibly futuristic Pudong. What a relief. I got lost in the French Concession (an area of the city), and as the sun peeked out from a clear patch of sky, light flakes of snow started falling. I was happy.

I ducked upstairs into a hairdressers to get a quick trim before catching a cab back to my hostel. It had a view of the bustling Bund and the familiar marks of Western colonialism: archways and manor-style doorways, clock towers and colonnades; stone buildings once housing financial institutions. From the rooftop bar, it was a surreal sight. Whole buildings across the river became televisions at night. An entire Times Square city.

On my second night at the Captain Hostel, I befriended Terry, a black girl from Manchester with short pink curls. She invited me and a group of travellers to an expat penthouse party, south of the city centre. The gathering was cracking along and the first thing I saw was a Chinese boy in baggy jeans and a military-patterned hoodie drinking Tsingtao on a couch. He cocked his head at me and smiled. Before I even met the host, he approached me and said hello, telling me I looked like Harry Potter.

I liked Jack instantly. We chatted in half-languages. He didn't know anyone at the party either. He had met the hosts on the street days earlier. They had stopped him to comment on his hoodie.

Eager to party, Jack and I gathered the crew and went to a bar in the French Concession. Judy's Too was a pole-dancing bar, very interwar Shanghai, chock-full of Mongolian prostitutes.

Jack and I drank vodka mixes and danced with our hoodies over our heads, all grinning and ghetto. We then sat in the corner. He was barely audible when he said, 'Can I kiss you?'

I thought twice. It had been six months since my false start with Jason. But I was only here for a couple of days; this was a new city, and I was in need of new-city fun.

His slow kisses had the same thoughtfulness as his smile. Terry cheered me from another corner and rallied the others from the hostel to watch. Jack and I took cover on the booty-shaking dance floor. The beats brought Jack alive and he consumed four drinks in quick succession.

After three hours Jack grabbed my head and whispered in my ear, 'I have a girlfriend.'

'Uh.' I closed my eyes, felt my chest deflate.

'Can we talk outside?' he suggested, and pushed me through the handbags and elbows to the door. We found a spot next to a factory, sheltered from the cold, wet street.

He leaned his back against the wall and let his plastic cup of alcohol spill onto the driveway. His lips were shiny with saliva. He was drunk and slurred, 'I like boys. I'm a freak. A freak.'

He dropped his head back against the brick and stared open-faced at the sky.

'That makes *me* a freak,' I said and pinned his shoulder to the wall with my hand to give him balance.

'You're gay?' His teary eyes focused on my face.

'Yeah. Of course,' I joked. 'Remember. We were kissing?'

He squirmed out of my hold and pushed me. 'I don't want to fuck,' he said in Chinese.

'Whoa. Chill out. Me too,' I said in English. 'That's not what I'm after.'

In Chinese again, 'I can't give you this, or this.' He grabbed his crotch then his backside.

'You're drunk', I gasped, feeling my throat tighten with embarrassment. 'I think I should go to bed.' I lurched to the taxi queue and pressed the folded paper containing my hostel's address into the driver's palm. 'The Bund,' I said.

In the morning, Terry bought me coffee and we read newspapers in the hostel foyer. My phone rang. Jack.

'James, I'm sorry,' he started. 'I'm not gay. I have a girlfriend. I love her. I'm sorry, but I was drunk and I lied to you.'

'Why did you kiss me like that?'

Terry moved into the seat next to me.

'I kiss my friends, we're brothers. I'm not gay and never will be.'

I dared him to come out for a drink with Terry and me later.

'If I can bring my girlfriend,' he replied.

Terry leaned into the phone to catch the conversation. We conferenced. 'I'm here darlin' boy. We're sor'ed,' Terry whispered in her pinched Mancunian accent. 'We'll have a fabulous night, orright?' So I said sure.

More bars. More alcohol. More and more Shanghai. Jack showed up with his girlfriend Helen, who was beautiful, shy and intelligent. She had a pale, flat face framed by black hair. A young corporate banker without any of the worldliness that implies. They held hands. Curiosity had replaced last night's embarrassment, and I suggested we go to some gay bars.

'That'd be *wick-ed*,' Terry jumped in, eyebrows arched and staring at our straight couple. She shook her boobs. 'Do you like dancing, honey?' she said to Helen and touched her forearm. 'Because I do!'

There were a few other gay people at this Irish pub, so we went in convoy out of town in search of what the local expat magazine described as a 'small gay live jazz venue with a local and alternative-minded crowd'. After half an hour of peering at numbers in a residential area of Shanghai, we spotted a two-star hotel. In the foyer an elderly couple was asleep with the TV blaring. We slowly opened the door and roused them.

'Do you know where this bar is?' I asked, showing the old man the Chinese script. He pointed at a red door to the side of the foyer, and somebody at the back of our group guffawed. We opened the door into darkness and the old man, who was only wearing thermal underwear, quickly turned on the lights to reveal a tiny all-red room with bar stools, one mirror ball, and a small selection of liquor on a dusty wall.

He pulled on his trousers and offered us a drink. Soon we were laughing so hard we had to leave; the old man was getting pissed off.

Our second attempt was more successful after Jack called ahead: Eddy's was a small and stylish bar in the style of Manhattan's upper west side.

Helen leaned across the table and whispered, 'Are you gay?'

'Love, baby. He's gay, I'm a dyke. It's a gay bar,' Terry beamed. 'We've been going to gay bars tonight. And we're going to more, darlin'! Do you want a beer?' She wiggled her way to the bar.

A song Jack and I heard at Judy's Too came on the speakers and Jack stared at me.

House was our next bar; a tatty mansion in the French Concession packed with shirtless men. Helen looked lost and stunned and went to the bathroom. Jack quickly gestured for me to follow him behind the cloakroom. He pushed me hard against the wall and pressed his mouth to mine.

'Jack, no,' I said, peeling his hand from my face. 'What are you doing?'

'What?' he complained and moved in again.

'Jack!'

He walked off to the bar and ordered a vodka.

Terry came up behind me and pinched my bum. 'One more dance, baby boy.' She pulled my face into her breasts. Then staring after Jack she said, 'We're blowin' these loverbirds off and movin' on up!'

I agreed and we left. I spent the rest of the night dancing with a Japanese guy who was very funny. I told him about Jack.

He laughed, and said, 'Fucking straight boys. Go find him tomorrow.'

I took a taxi to Jack's work just as he knocked off. He was standing at the reception of the Shangri-la Hotel Fitness Centre in his work tracksuit. He'd been there since 5.30 a.m. and he looked happy to see me, if tired. We stood dumb in front of the view of Shanghai. I felt like I was floating on an up-draught of hot air.

'I want to go somewhere before you leave to kiss you again,' he said finally. My plane left in three hours.

'OK,' was all I said.

I paid for another taxi to take us into the southern suburbs of Shanghai. Forty minutes later we arrived at Jack's house, a small apartment in a 1970s-style high-rise.

'Your mum is not home?' I asked. Her incense and shrine had just been used for afternoon prayer.

It was the feeling of entering an empty house when you're not supposed to be there. *Now or never*, I thought, but after our lips touched he pulled away and turned his head. I wanted to disappear.

'I've hurt you, I know that, and you should be angry,' he murmured. Jack slumped on his bed and we looked at each other for a long time.

'Why me?' I asked in Chinese.

'Because you're lovely.' he said in English. 'James West. He's a good guy.'

'Do you have sex with your girlfriend?' I had to know. Was he a *tongzhi* in denial?

'Yes. Last night,' he said. 'I don't feel that way about boys.'

'You said that you loved me when you first saw me.' I wasn't angry; I hadn't believed him then. I was testing him to find the truth.

'It's my fault. I have never met a gay person before. I have never kissed a boy before. I like kissing my boyfriends on the cheek to say goodbye. I don't know why you don't have a girlfriend. Everybody has a girlfriend.'

I didn't answer him. He put on Nirvana *Unplugged* and we sang along until I heard the door open and close and plastic bags rustle.

I was the first foreigner Jack had ever brought home. His mum was too nervous to speak, but she bowed and nodded as I left.

On the street I kissed Jack goodbye on the cheek and I went to the airport.

I missed being needed. I wanted to hug Jack in that single bed in that rainy city I didn't know, with his mother fussing in the next room. It didn't seem like an unusual thing for two lonely people to do.

Although most of China's north remained frigid and locked indoors, things were wet and thawing in Shanghai as I left it, blurred by angular streaks of rain. I wanted light. Winter wired me wrong. What was I doing? I felt that lurch, at once exciting and isolating, of being very lost in Asia.

Transit, having left but not yet arrived. Around me at Shanghai Pudong International Airport was the seamless, generic face of travel. Pictograms, timetables flicking over, voiceovers in two languages, the layout of security checks with metal detector wands.

Clicks and beeps constituted the international language of travel. Aeroplane safety, the smell of jet fuel, boarding calls, smoking rooms and prayer rooms to accommodate our vices, our beliefs.

I watched planes land and take off in the grey sweep of rain, arcing out beyond the imagined sea to the east. With place names boiled down to destinations, I could be anywhere, I could be anyone.

I took my melancholic reverie onto the plane but it was rudely interrupted by the man next to me. The *laoban*.

The *laoban* is a creature native to China. He is most often encountered on trains, planes and in taxi queues. *Laoban* is the name ascribed to a boss. A *laoban must* be male. He smokes. He has a knack for negotiation. He often takes long *baijiu*-fuelled lunches in restaurants with other *laoban*. They yell, a lot. A *laoban* owns an automechanic's workshop, is a landlord. He runs a travel agency; he has earned a pedigree but hammers out his respectability through good old-fashioned wheeling and dealing. He is a practitioner of the ancient craft of *guanxi* (you scratch mine; I'll scratch yours for a bit longer to ensure the scratching lasts a lifetime – a failsafe plan). A *laoban* has connections.

You didn't need to speak to a *laoban* to identify him. *Laoban*-wear is a uniform: a polo shirt, suit pants, pointy patent leather slip-ons, and a black belt with silver buffed-up buckle. The shirt is always tucked in, the pants always high. And always on the belt hangs a set of keys and a leather mobile-phone case. Variation is found in the colour of the slacks, a leather man-bag, the pattern of the polo shirt and the brand of mobile phone. Most of the clothing stores in China sell a full range of *laoban*-wear for their growing numbers. It was identikit-wear for an instantly recognisable peer.

I was moody. This *laoban* made me nervous. He wanted to know my opinions about flash issues between East and West. I didn't want to get trapped in an argument about things I knew we both had predictable views on. But this *laoban* was earnest. He had a newspaper and at each international headline wanted sparks to fly.

'You're a journalist, you read these things every day, you must have opinions,' he said, rotating his belly towards me. 'Do you think America is right in hating China right now?'

'I'm not American,' I said. 'And hate isn't the right word. It's politics more than pride. I think America expects China to come to the same party as everyone else, especially when China is making so much money.'

'But we are still such a poor country, and they are so rich,' he countered. 'We still have so much poverty and we are doing our best to give people a better life.'

He cleared some phlegm into a handkerchief the colour of dried blood, and went on, each of his words sombre. 'We don't hate the Americans,' the *laoban* said. 'We don't hate anyone. We are not racists.'

I disliked how both East and West framed this debate. Commentators conflated trade and racism and made the debate about national character rather than obligations recommended by international organisations.

At the time the big issues were US pressure on China to deregulate the yuan and China's dumping of cheap goods in the West, undercutting local manufacturers. I was no economist, and I had listened to all responses to this debate, including moderates and hardliners. Most said that China was doing a balanced job at slowly liberalising markets in line with international demands. In one interview with Bert Hoffman, lead economist with the World Bank in China, I had asked why China was taking such a back seat in the Doha Round of WTO meetings in December 2005. He was upbeat.

'It's been very successful because a lot of countries are now interested in investing in China and making China its production hub. They are no longer afraid of being excluded because of increases in tariffs and now China is, if you want, a much better partner for investment. By the end of 2007 basically everything is done.'

And I said as much to the *laoban*.

'What about the death penalty?' he then asked, out of the blue. A frisson shot through me.

'I think it's a huge waste of life,' I said. 'Nobody learns.'

In one year China executed four times the number of people than the rest of the world put together. Amnesty International says that in 2004, China killed 3,400 people for crimes ranging from murder to tax evasion and drug trafficking – 90% of the world's total, for a country with 20% of the world's population. I knew of the bullet tax, where families were required to pay for the bullets shot into prisoners' heads. I knew of shockingly short trials – and no death row. I'd heard of corruption. But I had done only cursory reading into the issue. I did believe, however, that no one nation could claim the exclusive right to kill its citizens without attracting international criticism.

The *laoban* smiled and carried on eating peanuts; his big face received several dabs from a serviette. 'We have a population that is not very educated, not like yours. People need to know what is right and wrong. They need to be told that evil is punished.'

Evil people need to be punished. Evil people?

'There is no evidence that the death penalty deters future crimes from being committed. I don't believe in evil,' I went on. 'I think we should be responsible for the causes of crime.'

'When our country is ready we might be able to stop killing for some crimes, but people need to learn.'

'I can't argue with you. I'm not Chinese. This is not my country,' I said, reaching into my bag for my MP3 player. 'But for me, it makes me . . . it makes me angry. I think it destroys families.'

'Families created these people,' said the *laoban*.

'And society creates family.'

I'd had enough. 'I might listen to some music. Is that OK?'

It was late, possibly 11 p.m., when my phone vibrated. It was Jack. Disembodied, his voice sounded more teenage. I had been expecting him to call. This would conform to pattern and I needed pattern. I had my routine prepared.

'Hey, how are you?' I tried to sound alert. 'What did you do today?'

'I worked. Are you working tomorrow?' he asked.

'Yeah. And you?'

'I gotta work at two-thirty in the afternoon,' he said.

'Excellent,' I said. 'You get to sleep.' It still smarted, what happened in Shanghai. I needed him to get to the point.

Jack paused. 'I am so sad that I can't sleep tonight.'

Aha. 'Why are you sad?'

He answered softly, 'My father has gone forever.'

I sat up. 'Forever? Where to?'

'He's dead. My uncle told me this morning. I did not know. Crime. He took drugs from Yunnan to Shanghai. He was killed by the government.'

PART FOUR

SPRING

CHAPTER 19

MAY WEEK

Jack has a big grin. When he laughs his eyes light up and narrow. He has a mischievous quietness. He prefers a look to a word, a wink over a joke. An hour without words and he still makes me laugh. He doesn't talk much, but his brain is always on.

At least, that's what he was like in Shanghai.

Jack has an open face. When he cries it's like something slowly fractures across it, like the surface of water breaking. It's a silent crying, the type where the chest doesn't heave, the hands don't clench, and it's not hard to breathe. It creeps across his face, and he lets it because this happens all the time.

Cups of herbal tea litter my bedroom floor. We talk. It's nearly four months since we kissed in the lantern-filled Shanghai bar. Now he hugs a pillow. Every time we're on the bus, or in a taxi, he hugs my backpack. 'I like holding things close,' he says later. He blinks out tears and looks at me. I don't want to touch his shoulder in support, or ask him if he is OK, or even wrap him in my own hug. That would be heavy. It would stamp at grief's delicate edges.

Jack is 23. I'm now 24. I have been to few funerals. My grandfather, my dad's dad, died when I was very young, he is something of a half-lit memory – I only recall park walks by railway lines, and a suburban garage full of tools. He occupied my childhood like a character in a book that was only real if I chose to believe. It was as if he didn't die. I simply grew out of him, like I grew out of Grade Three.

So I watch grief from the outside. I see my friends lose bits of themselves. I don't know what Jack is feeling. I can see wet eyelashes, pale skin, the way his body looks pinned, limp, to the corner of the room, pinned by gravity. His face has changed since Shanghai. He has dark circles under his eyes. Something has gone. I haven't seen his eyes light up and narrow for days.

It took a week for both of us to sit like this in my room. May Day holiday week, to be exact, one of three mad 'seven-day holidays' in China, though Chinese companies rarely let people off for the whole time. Employees are forced into overtime, working the weekend before to get the weekend afterwards off. The May Day holiday only became a seven-day event in 2000 when the government promoted it to the status of 'Golden Week' – a name that accurately describes its purpose to encourage consumer spending.

May Week was also a major travel period, like Spring Festival. This May the government commanded forty-eight new airports be built across the country over the next five years to cope with air traffic that will double over the same period.

I had been a traveller myself just before May Week, out of necessity rather than luxury. I had recently quit my job at CRI (more on that later) and was dealing with the bureaucratic fall-out.

There are two options when stripped of your visa. Option A: pay an agent to bribe someone in the Public Security Bureau. There are pros (staying in Beijing and feeling like you're in a cold war film) and cons (having your passport lost by the Chinese postal service or sold on the black market).

Then there's option B: go to Hong Kong where you could arrange a new visa for the mainland. I chose the latter, a well-trodden route for expats needing quick re-entry.

Hong Kong couldn't be more different from Beijing, and I needed a holiday. I saw it as an opportunity to get frisky on Western excess and from my first glimpse of the skyscrapers along Victoria Harbour, I knew Hong Kong would do the trick.

I didn't know how much until I went into a trendy café. Boys were wearing high-top Nikes, black-rimmed glasses, extra-large t-shirts and stovepipe jeans; the girls in breezy tops, shorts, colourful runners with a big mobile phone around their necks.

I ordered a muffin. I hadn't had baked goods in nine months. 'Would you like me to warm your blueberry muffin a bit, sir?' the waiter asked deferentially.

I almost purred.

'Oh yes,' I replied, watching him lift it with silver tongs and place it in a small oven.

'The butter is on the side for you, sir. Please enjoy our free Wi-Fi.'

Later – heady with purchases and hi-NRG beats – I discovered anew that a warmed-up muffin isn't the only great thing about Western capitalism. Pore-refining cleanser is another, as is men's shower gel with 'pH respect' and zinc enrichment. Spray deodorant too!

'Beijing?' I found myself thinking. 'What Beijing?'

With pores refined, I mooched from café to bar in the alleys off Hollywood Street and feasted in warrens of boutique eats. I read my first uncensored news in months in the *South China Morning Post*: they even made fun of President Hu Jintao. I could visit any website – BBC wasn't blocked, Wikipedia wasn't blocked. Freedom.

I walked the length of the island into Kennedy Town where 7-Elevens nestle alongside Cantonese antique dealers. Sitting on the harbour's edge, I looked out towards Sydney. The smell of salt, the advertising, the couples smoking on the piers – it all reminded me of home. It's amazing what a bit of spending does for a homesick Western boy.

But a day later I thought how money makes everything look the same: branded but banal. For all of Hong Kong's perks, I kept thinking how nice it would be to be back somewhere unique, where the price is always negotiable if you call the bartender your friend.

Only four days away and my Beijing was unrecognisable. Humans had finally exhausted Earth's resources and colonised

Mars. That's what it looked like. Sandstorms had hit the capital and the city was shrouded in orange. Visibility had shrunk to metres. Breathing became a chore.

The storms were conjured in the far west and unleashed on Beijing by strong winds. In the weeks before the May holiday, Beijing experienced its worst pollution levels in six years. State media reported that by April the city had had just fifty-six 'blue sky' days, sixteen less than the same period last year, and well short of Olympic targets.

In the aftermath of the winds, which picked up other, more sinister chemical dust on their trip from the Gobi, windows everywhere received a brassy, antique tint. I left mine open one stormy night, and the next day a matte film covered my clothes, my computer, my bed, and the inside of my lungs.

I developed a chronic chest infection. My lungs filled with gunky lumps of Beijing air and mucous. I barked a wet cough and nursed my growing paranoia about some fatal, airborne illness.

One morning, aroused with fever, I pressed a taxi driver wearing a facemask to take me to the nearest hospital. He opened the windows and stared at me wide-eyed in the rear-view mirror. He sped through the deserted streets. (These were the frenzied days of bird flu coverage, with daily reports of poultry culling in provinces close to Beijing. It was not unreasonable to suspect the racing pigeons roosting next door were flying time bombs.)

The driver dropped me off and gestured for me to put the money on the front passenger seat. His wheels made a cartoonish squeal and he was gone. Inside the hospital was evidence that the storms had led to a 40% surge in patients that month. Delirium magnified suffering. People pushed and yelled. Packs scrummed at a confusing series of windows for forms and receipts. The lobby was a hospice of patients propped up against walls, sitting on luggage. There was nothing in Roman letters anywhere and I could only recognise a handful of characters. I almost left, but at that moment hacked up a lung and fortified myself for the worst.

Without warning, I was picked out of the crowd by several fussy, plain-clothed attendants and conveyed past the pushing hordes, to a gently inclined ramp that led to a pretty alcove. The Foreigners' Wing. Inside, air-conditioning wafted through vents in the ceiling.

I looked around with a serene, sweaty smile.

Nurses in crisp white uniforms helped me with the perfunctory forms, after which a pleasant doctor with stunning English and manicured hands examined me. He did blood tests and I left with an armoury of Western and traditional Chinese medicines from the well-stocked pharmacy on the same floor. I had found a medical oasis in the middle of Mars.

A rainstorm broke as I left. The rain made the road blur and bounce white. The coppery smell of wet asphalt was rare in Beijing. Stormwater drains, surprised, spewed onto slick, dangerous streets. Drivers fiddled with windscreen wipers, called into action for the first time in months. Within moments, boys were pushing boxes of umbrellas on the footpaths for 10 kuai (80p) each, undercutting the magazine stands and the subway hawkers.

I took the long way home in a taxi because of flooding. We went through the CBD, mostly abandoned building sites, cranes set black against the blacker sky. For a moment the city itself – the buildings, the growth – simply stopped. A pause in the incessant conversation.

Beijing had been fiddling with the weather again. That day, Xinhua reported that state technicians had fired seven rockets and 163 cigarette-size sticks of silver iodide into the city's skies to induce rain. The Beijing Weather Modification Office promised to use this type of cloud seeding to clean the streets before the Olympics and ward off heavier downfalls for the actual event.

It was the heaviest rain that spring and it only lasted twenty minutes, but it was long enough to breathe out and take stock.

Jack had been planning to visit me for weeks. I was the only person he knew in Beijing. My flatmate Yoni was away in Gansu province, travelling the desolate countryside and relying on the endless hospitality of local monks, so I offered Jack a bed.

I met Jack at Beijing's main railway station on May Day at peak hour. I spotted him easily among migrant workers. Helen was there too, looking glum from the overnight train journey during which neither slept. They were too excited about coming to Beijing for the first time. I approached and Jack offered a hug. It was good to see him.

Helen hugged me too, though with nervousness. It was clear Jack had told her about Shanghai. I was glad Helen was there. Now I could put away those feelings permanently.

To my surprise, and delight, all the Shanghai gang came to Beijing that May Week, including Terry, the glamorous Manchester lesbian. It was a week of debauchery. We went to bars. We partied in Wudaokou, at ZUB. We partied in Sanlitun, at Kai. We took in some live music as well, a clutch of international bands at Yugong Yishan.

My liver began complaining after the third day of binge drinking. We developed and then nurtured various bad habits to full-blown maturity. Bad habits like pole dancing. Bad habits like drinking games in a bar with the slogan 'Shut Up! Just Drink!' in Houhai. My apartment was a hostel for the week. Terry was with me in my bed, sharing spooning responsibilities like a professional and developing theories on why gay sex was so much better than straight sex.

'It's all about the *face*,' Terry said, giggling from marijuana at 4 a.m. 'Don't you get it? It's *fabulous*. It's all about the face. Groin on face. Face on groin. That's the thing that unites gay sex, and makes it so much better than straight sex. It's about grinding groin on face and having your face ground by groin.' She repeated that last sentence over and over, faster and faster. 'Grind that groin and be ground!' she screamed.

The house was a tip of longneck Tsingtaos and ash.

It took a week, and all its drinking, for Jack and I to deal with what happened in Shanghai, and to be able to talk about his dad, about what happened when he was taken away from Jack only months ago.

BUT HE'S MY FATHER

Jack's father was a cliché of addiction. He was an alcoholic. He was a gambler. He would return home at night drunk, and hit Jack. When his mother tried to intervene he hit her too. Nobody in the apartment block or in Jack's extended family talked about the abuse. You don't talk about things like that in China. So things stayed the same for years.

'My father would always argue with my mum,' said Jack. 'He had no job and just wanted to gamble. I hated my father so much when I was a child. I saw my father punch my mum. She couldn't do anything about it. They argued with each other because of me. Sometimes if I didn't do my homework my father would slap me. My mother would try to stop him and so then they argued.'

'But he's my father,' Jack added, tapping the edge of his teacup. He would say this again and again – 'But he's my father' – as if this was the only way he could deal with the blame, the grief and longing. But he's my father. Jack's only chance to forgive him.

Gong Jin bet away any money he had on mahjong games in backroom dives. An unemployed silk-factory worker, broke, he hung out with bad people, including Jack's neighbours. He once tried his hand at running a hardware store, but it soon closed.

The bad times were terrible, but the good times kept the family together through to the next low. Jack would be showered in presents: clothes, toys, computer games, anything he wanted from

Nanjing Lu, Shanghai's biggest shopping arcade, a colossal stretch of brands. When Gong Jin was in a good mood he was affectionate with his wife.

At that stage, Jack was growing up in the Huangpu area, an older part of Shanghai near what is now a hemmed-in commercial district; like having an outhouse in the backyard, it was inconvenient to find the toilet at night. But the atmosphere was thrilling for a young Chinese boy, surrounded by neighbours and friends, alive to the bustle of night-time food stalls in the maze of streets adorned with washing.

One of Jack's favourite childhood memories is when his dad salvaged an old door from the *gong di* nearby (the vacant lot under construction) and brought it back into their small street. He balanced it on two chairs, flat, to create a makeshift ping-pong table. Children would gather around while Jack and his dad practised China's national sport. Jack's dad always won.

I told Ruixiang Guo, the boss of United Nations Development Fund for Women (UNIFEM) Jack's story when I met her in Beijing. I wanted to know how many children struggled through domestic violence.

A three-year survey released in 2004 by the government-run All Women's China Association looked at 270 million households. It revealed that three in ten women had experienced domestic violence. According to the study, nearly half the Chinese population believed it was acceptable to beat wives, and 44% blamed the women themselves for provoking unreasonable behaviour.

While domestic violence happens everywhere, among all classes of people, China's enormous rural-urban economic divide exaggerates the problem. Despite Mao's dictum that Chinese women 'hold up half the sky', in a country with already staggering suicide rates, Chinese women kill themselves at a rate twenty-five times higher than men, a quirk in global trends. Rural rates of suicide are triple that of the cities and domestic violence is seen as a leading cause.

Ruixiang's job is a difficult one, because despite outreach, lobbying and technical support for NGOs on the ground, there's no real way to measure how successful recent implementation of legislation has been. 'Sometimes we do see statistics,' she says, 'but what we can believe is very under-reported.'

Ten years ago, when Jack was growing up, it was considered an extreme loss of face to go public about violence in the home. 'Community support was almost zero,' Ruixiang says of the time before 1995. 'Even if people did know, they thought, "this is *your* business".'

Ruixiang says that even when young married women returned to their own family homes for safety, they were often turned away. 'Usually parents sent them back,' she says. 'Once you've married, you belong to that family. You have to be responsible for your own life.'

In Beijing in 1995, Hillary Clinton famously attended the Fourth International Women's Conference, after which a flurry of excited talk surrounded issues of legal rights for women. Over 300,000 people attended the conference and a document called Beijing Platform for Action was produced. Several provinces adopted new legislation. Hot-lines and counselling services were established. To date, Ruixiang says over twenty provinces have issued ordinances and bills covering domestic violence.

'I think the attitude towards violence – I *personally* think – that it's changing slowly,' she says. 'But if we keep silent it won't be possible to make a big difference.'

After twenty years of marriage, Jack's parents divorced when Jack was thirteen. Gong Jin moved out. Divorce carries stigma and Jack was teased and ostracised at middle school.

'In China if your parents divorce the other boys will say, "You don't have a father! You don't have any parents or religion,"' says Jack. They called Jack an orphan. He felt very different from his peers. But one orphan finds another quickly. Ma – another boy at school – had divorced parents too. Jack and Ma are still best friends today.

Jack's father moved to Yunnan in the southwest, the country's most lush and geographically diverse province. It is famous around the world for the Tiger Leaping Gorge, its ethnic minorities, and the Burmese border. Encouraged by a long-time family friend in Shanghai – who turned out to be the boss of a drug syndicate – Jack's dad became involved in the heroin trade, trafficking to Guangzhou and Shanghai. He made enough money to pay back debts, buy himself a nice house and set up a life in Yunnan. He remarried. Jack doesn't like the woman at all. 'I think she likes money more than my father does.' But then Jack never questioned the gifts from his father – a new phone, a TV, and a computer – after Gong Jin had moved to Yunnan.

Yunnan is the major gateway for drugs into China from the 'Golden Triangle', which lies along the Mekong River in Laos, northern Thailand and Myanmar (Burma) and is one of the world's most productive poppy-growing regions. Nearly 80% of the heroin seized in China in 2004 was produced there and smuggled across the border from the Muse and Kohkang areas of northern Myanmar. In 2001, to mark UN Anti-drug Day (much to the chagrin of the UN, I imagine), thousands of Chinese gathered in a stadium in the capital of Yunnan to watch twenty alleged drug dealers sentenced to death. The same happened all over the country in various public squares and stadia.

Jack's dad was successful in making money and evading the authorities for two years. He would even come back to Shanghai to visit Jack and his mum, though the real reason for the trips were shipments of drugs.

But one day in May 2005, this life caught up with him. Fortified by alcohol, Gong Jin couriered drugs to a Yunnan airport for what was now a routine operation. He was caught and arrested with two subordinates and thrown in prison. He became another statistic in China's crackdown on illegal drugs. He was one of 13,500 suspects arrested in 2005 for drug-related crimes in Yunnan, according to the Chinese National Narcotics Control Commission. The heroin he was carrying was added to a 5.19-tonne cache seized that year.

'I was shocked when I was informed by police,' Jack tells me about the airport arrest. 'I thought, *that's not real.* That's not my father. My father would never do this kind of thing. I didn't want to talk to my friends, I didn't want to talk to anyone. I just listened to music and stayed at home.' An already quiet boy, the news drove Jack to withdraw completely.

Over his time in prison, Gong Jin wrote ten letters to his Shanghai family. Letters were the only way to communicate. In one letter, dated 1 January 2006, Jack's dad seems unaware of his fate. He is almost philosophical in tone. The letter is addressed to Jack's mum, who at the time was quite ill.

> I have received all your letters. I was deeply moved by them. I want to say thank you. What I did hurt you and the family and I'm very sorry. I miss you and the whole family. But please don't worry about me and please take good care of yourself. Now you must live with a heavy burden. If you're not healthy, you won't be able to handle it . . . Things will get better and better only if you have good health. And please spend more time with my parents to look after them. And keep in good touch with my brother and sister-in-law, so if anything happens you can talk to them and ask for their help. We're a family, after all.
>
> Please take care of yourself and raise Jack to be a good person. Jack is not so talkative, but I think he's very smart. He's better than me. I believe he will be very successful with his talents.
>
> I'm well at the moment, don't worry about me. If I need anything, I'll buy it myself. As long as you and the whole family are fine, I feel happy and relieved.
>
> That's life.

On 8 February 2006, at the age of 49, Jack's dad was dead. He was shot in the back of the head with a police gun.

Not much is known about how executions happen in China. Only a handful receive coverage every year, for political effect. Usually it concerns a corrupt official, and the execution is celebrated in the media as proof of continuing endemic graft.

Executions for reasons such as murder and drugs are rarely reported, so Jack's dad went under the news radar. I couldn't find any evidence of his death in the press. I did see the green death certificate booklet, about the width and length of a small Bible, detailing the time and place of the death. It was stashed away with banknotes and miscellaneous forms in a tin in Jack's Shanghai apartment. It looked like any other Chinese government document, stamped with red stars inside, filled out in poor handwriting by some clerk. The Chinese stamp on the front was gold embossed. Folded up in it was a wafer-thin receipt of some transaction.

The process of executions is secret. According to one online account by an executioner in Henan province translated onto the fascinating blog, EastSouthWestNorth, the policeman practises for two days beforehand. If this one bullet doesn't kill straight away, there's a police doctor on hand to issue the coup de grâce. Photos posted on this website show the damage done by one of these bullets. The top half of the head is blown off, the body slumps in a ditch in an anonymous killing field. Practices differ from province to province, according to the blog. In some accounts, if the body is not claimed, it's plundered for organs. I didn't ask Jack about his dad's organs but I did ask whether the rumour that the police charged the family for the bullet was true. He said it was. I wondered whether this was the receipt folded up like a taxi docket in the death certificate booklet.

The black market price to buy a life from the Chinese government was 300,000 kuai. That's nearly £24,500, about the cost of a Toyota four-wheel-drive.

Jack's mum tracked down the Yunnan friend of the family in Shanghai, the one who had brought her husband into the drug ring, and demanded the cash. Of course, to save his own hide, the drug boss (who Jack named the 'BMW Boss' for his taste in cars) refused to come forward.

'I don't understand!' Jack exclaimed in a rare outburst. 'He was my father's friend!' For a moment his face contorted into the same expression of having just sucked a lemon. BMW boss did, however, send 200,000 kuai (£16,300), proceeds of the original sin being offered back as bribery. Everyone else chipped in – Jack's grandfather and his aunt and uncle.

But Jack's aunt convincingly argued against adopting any backdoor solutions. She thought them risky and liable to make the situation worse. In the full cast of regrets, this one features for Jack and his mum.

'Maybe my father would now be in Shanghai.'

Instead, with the money, the family hired a reputable defence lawyer in Yunnan. 'Even then, the lawyer told dad there was an 80% chance he would be killed,' says Jack.

The only glue keeping this whole confusing operation together was the letters.

Gong Jin wrote:

> You didn't tell me much about the lawyer and I wasn't sure myself so I was very worried, I hope you can understand. Right now you have to analyse whether what our lawyer told us is the truth or not. The case is not over yet; the judge who is handling my case has not yet talked to our lawyer. You can call the lawyer after you get this letter. The lawyer knows the judge. Just tell him to tell you the truth. At the moment only our lawyer can help us to change the execution into a fine. They haven't come to see me yet after the lawyers met on 7 December and I don't know why. Please write to me to keep me updated when you get any new information. If we just have to pay a fine, it is better if you go to pay the fine yourself to make sure everything is OK.
>
> Remember, no matter what happens don't forget to write

to me, otherwise I will lose my mind. You know my temper. I know I am sorry, now I am such a burden on you. You have a huge weight on your shoulders, you have to do everything by yourself and you have to take care of our son, too. I feel horrible. If they can change the execution I will use the rest of my life to take good care of you.

This isn't like the movies. There's no rule by law. No appeals. There's no protracted back-and-forth between judges, victims' families, community advocacy groups. Once the sentencing happens, the prisoner is dead within a few days.

The last time Jack saw his father was in the Yunnan prison. He had fifteen minutes. 'He looked fine. He wasn't worried. He thought he'd be OK.'

Jack never said goodbye.

Inexplicably, the family wasn't told until after the execution that it had taken place. Jack had received a phone call at work from his uncle. He then worked an excruciating nine-hour shift in the hotel gym before coming home to comfort a distraught mother.

Jack's uncle went to Yunnan to collect the ashes. It was the first time Jack saw his uncle cry in front of anybody.

Jack's dad had gone, just one of over 1,000 people killed in China in 2006, according to Amnesty International counts. Though that number, they say, is more likely to be around 8,000. Some say over 10,000. Nobody knows.

No personal goodbye, no group farewell. There was no funeral. Relatives gathered at Jack's apartment for a private dinner. His grandmother had thought it inappropriate to mourn publicly. The family closed ranks against the outside world with a lie that everyone told, even to themselves. It's still being told today.

'My grandmother said to me, "Your father died from cancer. That way it's easy for you to forget him,"' said Jack, gripping one of my pillows. 'I don't want anybody to know about this. I pretend he is alive, that he is working somewhere else. It's very hard.'

Jack can't talk about it with his mum because she starts crying, which makes him feel guilty. At night he has started to shout, listening to loud music and getting trashed in clubs. Anything to be someone else.

And that's why he kissed me at the Shanghai bar. To freak himself out, to give himself jolts. Like applying a defibrillator directly to the brain. Not to be himself. We've all wanted that thought. I felt I understood him now.

That afternoon I took Jack and Helen to the train station to go home. Helen had been sleeping all afternoon and looked groggy.

I hugged Jack and pulled his hoodie up over his head, giving it a rub. 'Look after yourself,' I said.

'Don't worry about me,' he said. 'I'm OK.'

That was the last time I saw Jack for over a year.

CHAPTER 21

A STRANGER
IN THE SQUARE

It's so ubiquitous it's boring. A travel snap I wouldn't look twice at because I've seen something like it so many times. It's probably the most common photo in China. An awkwardly framed, out-of-focus Chinese tourist in Tiananmen Square.

It's not a good or bad photo. It's not good or bad weather. It doesn't look hot or cold (maybe it's spring or autumn given the light jackets and long sleeves). It's the normal, washed-out grey of a normal, washed-out day. That monochromatic sky that sits above 90% of Beijing days sits above this one too.

Someone in the distance is flying a red kite by the Great Hall of the People. In front of this is the usual handful of tourists not doing much, because in the barren square there's not much to do but to feel very, very small. Or fly kites.

And in the foreground is a man who looks so incidental as to be a stranger to the person taking the photo. He's not the sort of man used to having his picture taken. But he's not uncomfortable.

He's not good-looking or bad-looking. He looks like someone you might vaguely know, from the corner store, or one of your parents' friends. A strangely familiar stranger. He is almost ageless (I guess around his early 40s), classless (he looks neither rich nor poor), and not unremarkably dressed in blue jeans, a black zip-up jacket and a grey turtleneck t-shirt.

The expression on his face is unreadable, his pose gives nothing away. We only know he's Chinese, a man and in Tiananmen Square; just a guy captured in a photo in the mundane routine of travel, to be packed away and never seen again.

Photo albums across China are stuffed with people posing in Tiananmen Square who have since died. But the photo is symbolic because of this man's surroundings. This man was killed by the apparatus that his surroundings symbolically celebrate.

It's the first time I've seen a picture of him. They look alike, Jack and his father. The same height. Clothes swim on them both.

Gong Jin, given his surroundings, looks to me now like nameless collateral in China's endless pursuit for order.

When I look at a map of Beijing, the part of me that likes stationery stores is impressed by its symmetry.

I could fold it along the lines to make a paper plane. It looks clean from above, and attractive, especially the weight given to its core by the concentric streets looping around the world's largest public plaza – Tiananmen Square – at the city's centre. Jack's dad stands in the square, which houses the embalmed and entombed communist leader who built Tiananmen into what it is today.

Tiananmen and Tiananmen Square are two different things. Tiananmen – The Gate of Heavenly Peace – is the grand red gate at the Forbidden City's main entrance. But its meaning has changed. Tiananmen, the gate, now belongs more to the square outside the palaces than it does to the palaces themselves. Mao stares out from Tiananmen upon his square, his vast, flag-stoned emptiness. He owns the square and everything in it. There's an eerie dialogue between Mao's eyes and his mausoleum; he watches over his own dead body. I feel like I'm trespassing on a grave.

Tiananmen Square needed to be 'big enough for a billion', said Mao when he expanded it at the birth of the republic in 1949. But no matter how many people gather there these days, it still feels empty compared to the pictures of the Red Guards assembled during the Cultural Revolution (500,000 when the Revolution started), or the dense fête of the Tiananmen Square demonstrations of 1989 (over one million people by the end of May).

Big enough for a billion – a way to describe Tiananmen as the symbolic home for the entire story of the Chinese people – is plenty big enough to make one person feel meaningless.

The modern Tiananmen contains this essential contradiction of space in Beijing. This contradiction governs the entire urban design of the city. The promise, the *illusion*, of public accessibility jarring with symbolic order. The square is effectively an island, accessed only through a handful of tunnels (bleak tiled corridors of florescent light). You can't cross the roads.

People don't stroll through on a Sunday afternoon enjoying the light. There are no alfresco cafés spilling out into it like the European cliché, or musicians, or artists. The square is a destination rather than part of the journey.

It still amazes me that such emptiness can contain such political tension. Like a schoolyard during summer holidays, the square's emptiness only serves to divine memories from the stones. As a foreigner this means the mind imagines its own 1989 and paints it vividly in the space.

In my mind, played out across the grey expanse, I see a fight by people my age. I fill the space with chants and music, with posters and slogans, with life. Though I wasn't even remotely involved, as it is now the square feels like revisiting the site of a first date many years later, hoping to be struck by some critical or lost memory, only to be delivered shapeless nostalgia.

These days the largest thing that moves in it is regular and fatalistic: a digital countdown clock to the opening of the Olympic Games in 2008. It's fitting that it's here in Tiananmen. Historian Wu Hung argues that its proximity to Mao's mausoleum ties up a story of progress, a history that reclaims the square for the official story, once again.

I itch to leave, or to beat at the stones. I can only stay for fifteen minutes before needing to be somewhere else, somewhere

I can sit, out of the shadow of China's official struggle for order and identity.

The Forbidden City, north of Tiananmen, provides the other focal point of the capital. If Tiananmen Square is the socialist ideal of uniformity, the Forbidden City is what has been allowed to be preserved of the past. A UNESCO-listed site, it's another of Beijing's 'biggest things in the world' – the biggest palatial complex, with the biggest collection of wooden artefacts. It has 800 buildings and over 8,000 rooms.

It is a full day's exploration into the private lives of emperors past, and the scale of this once-secret world is truly forbidding. Tourist groups make the bigger pavilions like the Hall of Supreme Harmony unbearable, but there's peace to be had in the winding terraces of Zhongshan park dotted with Chinese pines. Even so, the Forbidden City's history as a walled-off and exclusive club for concubines is impossible to shake; the sense of the 'untouchable' remains.

To reach its centre, one needs to cross a guarded bridge under the luminous face of Mao, buy a ticket and move through and out of the centre again. The value in coming here is touristic only.

Order radiates around the Forbidden City in the form of the six ring roads, Beijing's traffic exoskeleton. It's as if someone has dropped a cage on the city from above and that's where it stayed. Six unforgiving structures that serve the cartographer's eye for symbolism (the Forbidden City and Tiananmen Square remain at the heart of the city) more than they do sensible traffic solutions. Because these arterial networks are themselves monuments, at odds with the natural rhythms of the city.

These natural rhythms can be found in people's communities: the comings and goings of bicycles, delivery men, shopping carts and children, the reptilian scales of traditional *hutongs*. For these rhythms, Beijing is an obstacle course. Ring roads slice large swathes of *hutongs* into quadrants, containing human movement or re-channelling it along overpasses and carriageways that flow out of the city. At times the ring roads draw a journey to a halt with unwanted exits and off-ramps. Pedestrians stand no chance against the brute design of this place. They can never cross roads where they want to. Beijing is about fences, pedestrian bridges, gates and walls.

The result is tension, a physical tension, but also a tension of identity. Most people don't know the name of a street only a few blocks away, or where a local museum is; these places don't exist as part of their Beijing. Walled in, locked down, and with attention directed to the great architectural performance of order at its centre, Beijing is a showcase that people just happen to live in.

That photo, and the man in it, summarises this for me. Tiananmen Square – as it has done before – washed its hands of the existence of Gong Jin, Jack's dad. Tiananmen Square will never remember him. The symbolism aches all the more for that moment's sheer ordinariness.

He has left Tiananmen – like the China it represents – without a trace.

CHAPTER 22

THE SHANGHAI BUS

I thought I would never fall in love with a city this ugly. I love it with something like lust: *I need it and I want it to make sense to me so I can't keep my hands off it*. I stick around because the promise of Beijing – and China – is too big to give up.

My parents think my relationship with Beijing is a hotheaded teen romance. They wonder when I might find a *nice city*, instead of this unwashed hulk.

'You don't understand,' I say. 'If only you could see what I'm see-ing, how good it can be sometimes.'

They point out that the city has a catalogue of offences the length of the Yangtze. It's rude when it's hot, and it's unrelentingly needy when it's cold. It never says sorry with a big parade or some free outdoor concerts. Instead the signs in the park read Keep off the Grass. It snores loudly at night.

'Besides, it doesn't love you,' they say. And they are right. Beijing never smiles for me. We never have moments that are ours alone. I hate it so much sometimes, and I call my friends to bitch. They want me out of this relationship, too, but I can't leave right now, too many mysteries are still unsolved. I sign up for another month, wondering if I'll ever truly leave.

My friends here tell me I'm developing Beijing syndrome, like Stockholm Syndrome, so named after a case in Sweden where hostages fell in love with their captors, despite the dangers their captors presented. But Beijing doesn't care whether I stay or go. The one similarity to Stockholm Syndrome is that I would defend Beijing well after my release, defend it with a loyalty that it doesn't deserve.

There is another appeal about coming back to Beijing, more honest, more visceral than any talk of politics and economics and change. Beijing is hedonistic. Beijing dirty-talks me into submission. It whispers in my ear, 'You're in your 20s, James. Let's have fun, baby, let's get wrecked. You know you want to.'

Sluts give good head, they say, and Beijing is no different. When I party with this city, it has me gagging for more. It will get me high or stoned cheaper than any other city, for twice as long, with twice the number of hot people. It will introduce me to DJs, artists, film-makers, and drop me in a restaurant with five famous actors all buying me drinks. It will keep the clubs open till dawn for me, when it will force another half down my throat so I can forget about sleep. Just when I'm coming down and craving intimacy, it will push me onto the dance floor and offer sex instead of love and tell me – *lie* to me – that they're the same thing.

The next Friday night I'll be ready to be felt up by my city again. To be bent over for another round of Beijing blur.

I love Beijing for its quirks and contradictions, as well as its carnality. Contradictions like seeing a migrant worker shower in the fountain of an upscale shopping mall, and quirks, such as going to Beijing's fake beach.

Twenty-five kuai (£2) on warm weekends meant access to 4,500 square metres of sand, three water slides and a volleyball set-up in Tuanjiehu park, tucked in behind the East Third Ring Road.

Wave machines in the main pool entertained teenage lovers in inner tubes for hours. In the shallow end, grinning kids bobbed in swimcaps and they giggled in the spray from a red, polka-dotted mushroom in the centre of the park. All the water slides had long queues of goose-pimpled flesh. Hundreds turned out on a Sunday, in bathers made of coarse fabric in a fantasia of colours. Fat *laoban* ate *chuanr* (skewered meats). Kids pissed on the fake, hollow rocks and built elaborate sand-things. There were a few girls in bikinis and high heels posing for studly youngsters. It was so strange, this Malibu pocket, hemmed-in by apartment complexes and one of the busiest roads in China.

Me and Scottish Jenny and Yoni my flatmate pretended to be sharks and then dumped each other in the water. Yoni held me in shoulder stands. Jenny and I conspired to dack his boardies. On the beach, we got sunburned, drank Tsingtao, ate hot oranges, and joked about sex and love and relationships.

'Everyone in Beijing has someone that they really should be with but they're not,' Yoni said. Beijing made you say things like that.

What Beijing had taught me about love was as addictive as the city's rate of change. It was the city of strange love. Love was always obscured by the possibility of flight. Love was either cross-cultural, or transcontinental. In such a crowded city, and with the sun beating down on this surreal beach, love became even more romantic, even more alien. Either we compartmentalised love so we could live without it, or we binged on love like hungry puppies, never knowing when we might be fed again. The absence of love made us crave it even more.

In Beijing, we understood why so much of the word *belonging* was made up of the word *longing*.

'James-boy, are you really back in China? Come stay with me in Shanghai!' Jack texted me soon after I arrived, back for a break between university semesters in New York, where I'd gone to study.

Within two weeks I was on a plane with Jenny to Shanghai, something of a work trip for us both. I went to see Jack again because he's been a key to my understanding this country. But on a trip to the Whore of the Orient, a few nights of fun couldn't be ruled out either.

I lived Jack's life with him for three days in Shanghai. Jack's China is different from my China. Jack's China is about buses. It is about timetables and scrumming for hours. It is about trips travelling from Pudong, over the Huangpu Bridge, the spine that links Shanghai's brain with its body.

The commute is stressful and people are grumpy. The skyline of Pudong throbs the closer we get, evidence that some Shanghainese have the highest standard of living in the country. The tallest hotel in the world is here. The new IFC building will be taller than this, the tallest building in China. *Everything* is taller, bigger and shinier.

Jack's Shanghai is different from my Shanghai, too. For him, Shanghai is not the Whore of the Orient, used for decadent play. Shanghai is hot, humid and crowded. A place defined by ambition, it can be cruel to failure. In this way Shanghai has more in common with Mumbai or New York than it does with the rest of China.

Living with Jack is a reality check. He's on the outside of Shanghai. Jack's bus carries him into the expensive city, where he can't afford anything. Jack needs to scrape coins together to get a beer and noodles. Running out of money is common. In his China there are no foreigners – not in outer Chinese suburbia, or in the tiny Qinghai restaurant where Jack eats breakfast.

It's not that the China dream has been lost or marred. It's just out of reach. Over an hour out of reach – by bus.

The bus trips do, however, give us a chance to talk about the year that has passed. Jack is happier now, but still very quiet and watchful. He says I can write about his father. It no longer makes him feel ashamed. Twelve months have helped him grow. He counts our week in Beijing last summer as one of the best in his life. And he has a new sense of freedom from travel, making new friends and becoming independent.

Life has improved, even though he doesn't have a job and if he didn't hate the police before, he does now. They accused him of stealing 17,000 kuai (about £1,400) from a Taiwanese business-man staying in the hotel where he worked. The hotel blamed Jack because he was the new guy. But Jack didn't even know where the keys were kept.

The police wanted an easy confession and even wrote one for him. Jack refused to sign it. He was held in prison for seven hours, and when he was released he quit. He was angry. Now he is poor and unemployed, again. He needs to help support his pensioned mother and a growing drinking habit of his own. (What else is there to do when you're whiling away the days in the grimy hangouts of Shanghai's suburbia?)

It's hard for Jack to get a job. He studied organisational manage-ment at an institute associated with an Australian TAFE, but to no apparent end. (He wouldn't steal, but he cheated in exams to pass.) Even with his certificate, Jack doesn't really stand a chance against the competition without a better tertiary education. I had learned that from my CRI colleague, Wong Xiaoke.

On Shaoning Street for another meal, I realise that Jack is nor-mal, but normal in a way that has little to do with the classic China on television, in the history books or in the media.

Amidst this clutch of cheap restaurants in the old city, we form a tableau that could be in any part of the world: young people like us interested in music and Western pop culture, enjoying drinking and making friends.

For the first time I can see more similarities than differences in China. The language of our consumer culture is universal. Shanghai is not so much a place. It's a mindset, and one that is very familiar to me. Jack – in the same way Shanghai became famous – wants to be global, overnight. He wants to know everything about the world, overnight. He wants to know about youth culture in London and Paris, overnight. This is Shanghai's norm: one foot inside China, one foot firmly in the world.

We sit as dark shadows of Shaoning Street. It's late. Jack hangs out with his best friend like I hang out with mine. Ma, an insomniac guitar player in a string of unsuccessful acts in Shanghai, loves Jack. We would call Jack and Ma 'blokes' in Australia. They drink beer, smoke cigarettes, and talk about masturbation, a lot.

'I sometimes do it twice a day to pictures of girls in their underwear. Or Avril Lavigne. I'm not interested in sex anymore with Helen. It's boring. It's the same every night,' he laments. 'I tell her that I don't want to. So I jerk off a lot.' Jack is trying to impress me with the unhinged boy chat. He is still very committed to Helen.

Ma 'hits the aeroplane' too now, since his girlfriend dumped him and broke his heart. He might turn gay, he jokes, and again I'm surprised by their lack of homophobia. They rib me about liking guys, but it's affectionate. Being gay is just one of the things they must accept if they are to accept the swag of other Western influences.

They talk about Nirvana, The Cure and Radiohead. Ma likes the Sex Pistols. Smoking and angsty, bewildered by the behaviour of women, and into punk music – it's all a very familiar, male scene. I squat comfortably next to them and for a while there's no sense I'm a foreigner. We roll together, Jack and I, that's what it feels like.

We go to a jazz bar in a basement where the host takes us right to the front. Ma and Jack know her. It doesn't strike me as unusual, the contrast of Ma's unwashed hair and hunched shoulders, Jack's passive, plain face, and the host's ballgown. The night reads like a Bret Easton Ellis novel but without its bitterness. We drink more beer and the boys talk about breasts. We watch stilettos stalk The Bund through the high basement windows.

I invite Jack to stay in the spare bed in my hotel while Jenny is away working, and we listen to *OK Computer* by Radiohead. With enough beer and great food I'm back to watching Jack's face and identifying him as *my* China.

Yet Jack isn't eloquent, about grief or politics. He mumbles. Often he doesn't want to talk. Often he gives up when he finds it difficult to explain how he feels. But he's OK, like he said he would be. He is a real person, a young man defined, and limited, by his surroundings.

Helen had had an abortion the previous year. I learned this on another long bus trip to the Shanghai Engineering University Annual Graduation Variety Show. It was my second night in Shanghai.

Jack doesn't always use condoms and Helen doesn't take the pill and no one could know about the pregnancy. If Helen's parents found out, the relationship would be over. So Jack and Helen saved the 1,050 kuai (about a month's salary for Jack) for the termination. Abortion is very common in China. The Chinese Ministry of Health said that over seven million Chinese women had abortions in 2005, though that figure doesn't factor in private hospitals or the morning-after pill, which the one-child policy has made widely available and comparatively inexpensive.

The show was on campus, an hour northwest of the city in amongst bewildering Euro-inspired multiplexes.

A graduation gala would never be part of my China, but Jack knew a lot of students and it was free entertainment for a night. Two of Jack's friends were performing in the show and I met more of them in the Hogwarts-esque annexe.

'Edison,' one said, shaking my hand. 'Thomas Edison.' He was a chubby guy in a cowboy hat. Ma was there too, and a singer who introduced herself as Elena. She wore tiny commando shorts and a see-through nightie.

We took our seats in the main hall. As the lights went down, spots and gobos swirled on the backdrop and a girl clutching a teddy bear began a graceful solo dance routine. She was soon joined by a throng of primary-coloured dancers for a spectacular routine performed to electro beats; an acrobatic, gravity-defying human pyramid was its climax. What followed was two hours of diverse acts. There was classical dance, a version of *liang zhu* (the Butterfly Lovers), China's famous tragedy of two lovers in the fourth-century Jin Dynasty who are not allowed to marry. After the hero dies of a broken heart, the heroine falls into his grave and the two become butterflies. Here, the two dancers were women. It was scandalous and had the audience of several hundred in stitches.

There was breakdancing from a group of boys in singlets. Between the acts were short films about the graduating class of 2007. The audience reacted loudly with waves of chatter, gasps and cheers. Elena got a rock-star reception for her Cranberries-like singing. Ma sang a sad song about loneliness, and glow sticks waved in time. In all, a very successful concert.

But Shanghai kids have long nights, so we went back into the city for food and beers.

At 5.15 a.m., Thomas Edison stumbled through the hallway of my hotel room with Ma and Jack, saying that they need to stay with me. They were steaming drunk. 'Please don't ask me to tell you why,' Jack said. 'We can sleep in the bathroom.' Thomas Edison was still wearing the cowboy hat. He fell against the wall; his face was sweaty and he reeked. Ma looked like he was about to vomit. I said that Jack could stay, but not the other two. There was no way I was letting the stench of three drunken boys disturb Jenny's sleep.

Ma picked up Thomas Edison and they made their way out into Shanghai, where it was already light. Jack crashed in my bed.

'What happened?' I whisper.

'Helen doesn't like me staying with you, cos you're gay,' he replied. 'We had a big fight about it. I didn't want to tell you because you would be upset. I told her I trust you. We're like brothers.' He passed out.

On my final night in Shanghai, we ate on a small street thick with the exhaust of hotplates. The street was lit by strings of naked light bulbs. Vendors sold bright red crawfish by the *jin* (a half-kilo). Others sold skewers of anonymous-looking sea creatures from deep dishes of seasoned broth.

There were towers of *xiao long bao*: soft, small dumplings filled with pork and hot soup that are the tastiest snack on Earth. First, make a small incision with your teeth to suck out the soup so it doesn't dribble everywhere. Then shove the whole thing in your mouth to get the rich, savoury explosion. Good, fresh *xiao long bao* bursts open then melts like a meaty mouthwash. Delicious.

After dinner and beers, Jack and I went back to his apartment. He had asked me to stay on my last night in Shanghai. It was my second visit there, but this time I had no more complex motives; it was cheaper. Jack's mum was asleep in bed with the television and the lights on. For the first time, I noticed the house was filled with weird stuff. A bronze horse. Fake plastic flowers, everywhere. Ornaments of every kind hanging from light fittings.

Jack's bed was hard and small and the Shanghai mosquitoes were warriors. He still had a poster of Avril Lavigne, and of the pretty-boy South Korean hip-hop band Click-B, over his bed. The piles of *dakou* CDs were still there too.

But what was new was, 'Kurt built his own world where I found myself', scrawled across the wall in permanent black marker. So too, 'Kurt Cobain was an amazing artist'.

Jack fell asleep right way. I stayed awake thinking. I wondered if I would have continued my friendship with Jack if I hadn't known his story. Probably. But I'll never, ever be sure.

I looked over at him sleeping, hugging his pillow, a wisp of a boy. He was smaller now, he wasn't eating properly. I drifted off to sleep thinking about how to do right by my subject and friend, thinking about his future.

Two weeks after I left Shanghai, Jack finally got a job offer from another hotel. He didn't take it. 'The schedule isn't very reasonable,' he texted me. 'And the bus doesn't come by my place.'

CHAPTER 23

ZAI JIAN, CRI

The day I quit CRI I felt I finally understood the place. It was eight months into my twelve-month contract and I was producing terrible radio. Pop music had ceased to sustain me on the daily subway journey. The weather was warming up but with unpredictable snow flurries. Babaoshan was bleaker than ever. I wasn't learning. I wasn't sleeping. I wasn't seeing China. I wanted out.

Heading home after my last day at CRI, the darkness of the taxi's back seat enveloped me. If going to Babaoshan was going to die, then leaving Babaoshan was meant to bring me back to life. But I was confused.

From the back seat, I gazed at the CRI building. It looked blank and impenetrable and I felt panic at never being allowed back in. I watched it shrink and finally disappear as I headed east, downtown, over flyovers and into the city.

It had taken some time for me to muster the courage to quit, and I received conflicting advice about how to go about it.

The advice from Stephen (while helping him chop carrots at his Wudaokou apartment): Bend the truth a little. Tell them you're taking up study and that you will need a few months for preparatory reading. Study is the holy grail of excuses. You wouldn't believe what I've gotten away with by a little email here, a little email there.

The advice from Scottish Jenny: We can be struggling freelance writers together and go shopping all afternoon! But seriously, I think the truth – just slightly tweaked – may be the best approach. Say you don't want to leave CRI in the lurch (you have really enjoyed working there blah blah) and so you've tracked down wonderful replacements who you can bring in for the Captain to scrutinise.

I *was* fearful of Captain Rorschach and of ruining the relationship between the ABC and CRI, which was about much more than just me. It had already grown sour after CRI fired one Australian on exchange; now they were going to lose their second.

If I broke my contract, I was up for a $2,000 fine, the cancelling of my flight home and the stripping of my visa. These were hefty penalties, though it was tougher for Chinese staff to quit. They were forced to pay around 20,000 kuai if they broke their contracts during their first six years.

Still, I *hated* the job: the four lifts and the way the doors would crush you if you hesitated a fraction too long at level five; the guards who checked my pass at the front gate, with me thinking, 'Why else would I be coming all this way if I didn't work here? You all look 16 and should do something about those zits.'

There were many niggly things, but what I really began to hate was the afternoon programming, where we were subjected to language-learning lessons outsourced to loony radio producers. Whacky learning scenarios were performed in hyped-up voices; whizzes and bangs emphasised key points. A helium-induced voice would exhort, 'Learning English is fuuuuuun! Weeeee!' A man would respond to new words with, 'But what does that meeaaan?'

I even asked Captain Rorschach if we could turn the office radio off for the afternoon since we could all speak English. 'If you don't want to listen to the radio,' she snapped, 'perhaps you shouldn't be working in radio.' (Another encounter around this time was at a farewell party for a retiring employee. The Captain was tipsy on pink champagne and she called me fat.)

Perhaps Rorschach was right for once. Perhaps I shouldn't be in radio.

I picked my moment on a quiet, windy Monday afternoon. I dry-retched in the bathroom first. I slapped my face with cold water and wrote notes on my palm while leaning against the bathroom wall. If I forgot how to speak, I could refer to some words: notice, replacements, tough decision. (Minutes later my palm had sweated so much it was black with ink.)

We were in the same room as our last stoush, and I remembered her yelling.

This time Rorschach picked a leather couch to perch on. Her feet didn't touch the ground. She was like a child sitting in her father's work chair. I could see that her black socks were pulled up to the same height on both legs.

'So,' she said, and folded her hands in her lap. Her hair hung just above her thin eyes. Her skin was tight around her jawbone. Her mouth was small. She showed no emotion. 'What are we talking about today, James?'

I sat down opposite the Captain and leaned forward, holding the printed CVs of possible replacements. 'Madam,' I rushed, 'I've decided that I want to leave CRI sooner than expected. I'm here to give my notice. An opportunity for study has come up.'

I tried to gauge her reaction before going on. She usually attacked, then offered conciliation. But today her face didn't move. 'I can stay until the end of the month to help you find another person,' I continued. 'I'm really sorry to cause any difficulty. But I think it's right.'

I waited for Rorschach.

She finally spoke. 'Well,' she said. Her mouth tried to form another word. She moved her hands to the arms of the couch. She looked at the papers in my hand. She then said, 'Of course. So what are we going to do? You've already made this decision.'

'Yes, it's final,' I said.

She stared from under her stiff fringe. I didn't breathe. Her index finger twitched.

'So you'll quit?' she said.

'Yes, Madam.'

'I see.'

'I will leave at the end of the month. And I have found some replacements for you.' I placed the resumes on the table. Rorschach flinched and for a moment looked ginger. She didn't pick up the papers.

Rorschach looked trapped. The week before, she had publicly promised that no foreigner would be fined if a contract had to be reviewed – she did this as a ploy to get a new employee to sign. She knew I would remember this. But I could detect a shift behind her eyes.

'And on what authority will you stay in China?' she said finally, a seeming afterthought.

'Authority?' I asked.

'Yes, yes,' a flicker of irritation crossed her face. '*Authority*. On what authority will you stay in China?'

My mind raced. 'I will work that out before the end of the month. You don't have to worry about that,' I said.

'You're right. I don't have to worry about that. I have enough to worry about as it is. But I don't have to worry about that. Once you're gone you're gone.' Her voice was clipped. 'So. I will talk to the Foreign Experts Bureau about your status here in China. And will get back to you.'

I had expected they would strip me of my visa, but the reality of it still shocked me.

'And when we work out your status we will talk to you again.'

My status. These words stuck in my head.

'OK, thank you Madam.'

She lifted the sides of her mouth and showed her yellow teeth. Rorschach collected the papers and briskly exited the room, leaving me shaken, but relieved. I felt as if I could have run a marathon.

My last day at CRI was also my best. Wang Lu bought me a lavish banquet at the CRI restaurant. My workmates came and gave me CDs and a plate and a mug adorned with the Chinese year knot (it was my year, the year of the dog). It was a decent-sized mug, too. It would be my writing mug.

I was expecting a barney with the Captain. On Scottish Jenny's last day the Captain had called her 'boyish' and told her she needed to be more womanly if she wanted to get anywhere in life. The Captain used last days as an opportunity to critique character. I was expecting a diatribe about loyalty.

Instead, Rorschach took me aside to express her personal thanks. She got so close I could smell her hairspray and the grandma odour of her clothes. She had slightly sour breath. I realised then just how old she was, and how small.

'If ever you want to come back to CRI, even to China, please let me know,' she said. This time her face was softer, more expressive. 'We will organise tours for you, whatever you want. Thank you so much for all your hard work. You've done a lot, everyone has told me this. Made so many contacts, and taught people so many things. I just wanted to say thank you, you intelligent boy.'

I was nonplussed, and returned to the feast. I dashed from table to table. There was laughter as stories were told of language, travel and on-air mishaps, the three things that bound us all.

In the taxi heading back into town, with an aria from Verdi's *La Traviata* gently playing in the background, I called Scottish Jenny.

'Don't let go of this feeling right now, hold onto it, because it makes a lot of sense,' she told me. 'For one day you feel like you have underestimated the place and you ask – have I made the right decision? And everyone is so nice, you forget all the annoying things they do, all the feedback they don't give and all the reasons you hate it.'

'But I regret that I might have misjudged the place,' I said.

'It's so true of CRI generally,' Jenny pointed out. 'It starts off so good. You feel like you are smack bang in the middle of things, in the very middle of China, broadcasting to China – this enormous and possibly brilliant country – and when you look back you realise how much work you've done.'

'You did fifty-something shows?'

'Fifty-two half-hour dialogues with fifty-two people who had to be interesting. Where did they all come from? And also, James, think about it. You and I both have broadcast to the most people we ever will in our careers. Millions in China, India, Pakistan.'

'CRI was everything. It was my China for so long. I got off the plane one evening, stumbled around Tiananmen Square for a day, then I was at work. That was it.'

'And apart from one or two Chinese friends you met under your own steam, everything else was off-limits. Integration is the worst thing that could happen in Rorschach's book. If you go out and live in the real China, the real thing and meet—'

'—you might find out what China is all about, or maybe even have more questions,' I finished for her.

'Exactly! Remember the enforced image of China that they gave us in those first months. They looked after everything, our visas, our housing, and our impressions.'

Just then, the back seat flooded with light as I passed the National Grand Theatre, the Great Hall of the People, then Chairman Mao at the front of the Forbidden City to my left, with its retinue of army officers and glare of red, and Tiananmen Square on my right. I felt as if I was slipping out of the middle of things as we sped past down Beijing's main boulevard.

It was a thrill to have been so connected to something like China Radio International. Right then I felt like I understood the grandeur of China, not just the surface of things – all that pomp, all that politics that can so alienate and awe the average traveller here.

'It's amazing, Jenny. Really. I'll see you tonight. Japanese behind the Hilton?'

As the taxi drove further away from the centre of China's government, part of me felt as if I was leaving China, that I'd forfeited what I came here for – a privileged insight into the world's biggest nation on the brink of becoming the world's next superpower. I could never go to Tiananmen again without feeling that secrets I once knew were being kept from me. Mao, like Mona Lisa, would smile enigmatically whether I was there or not.

The CD had switched from Verdi to Puccini's *Turandot* as I was nearing my apartment. A night out with friends and a new freedom. It all felt very significant.

It's one of life's strange twists, that you feel like you truly belong at the moment of departure.

PART FIVE

SUMMER

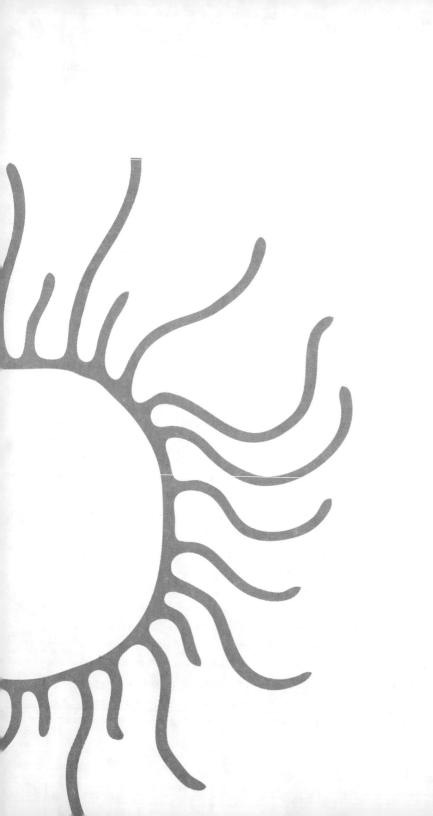

CHAPTER 24

BEYOND THE BLUR

It was time to see some of China beyond the borders of its two largest cities before I said my goodbye. Longsheng, in Guangxi Zhuang Autonomous Region in China's south, caught my fancy for no reason other than it wasn't Beijing.

The southern provinces were splitting with colour. It was summer again.

The renowned Longji Dragon's Backbone terraced rice fields are located outside Longsheng. But it was the town itself, a dense parade of shabby tenements along a tributary of the Li River, population around 150,000, that I loved. That this ramshackle city, crawling around the river and up the mountain, was in the same country as the geographically supine, yet politically erect Beijing surprised and excited me. This rice-paddy poverty.

Later that night I walked around the town looking for food but most restaurants had shut, as they do around eight o'clock or so. Chairs were up on the tables and teams of young cooks with loosened uniforms were smoking and digging into giant bowls of soup, rice and noodles. I found a dumpling place selling freshly steamed pork buns and chatted with some students out late about learning English.

If Beijing was worried about stability in the countryside they would find no challenge here from cultural inconsistency. In the shops there were the same gangs of teens in white jeans and shiny button-downs glued to CCTV's pulp soap operas and revolution-ary period dramas, the same government certificates hanging in the *wang ba* (the internet café), the same shopgirls asleep on the stand-alone freezer units in the mid-afternoon boredom. There were Mao posters in the workers' quarters of building sites and police banners instructing locals of the proper behaviour towards the elderly. Beijing was China's conscience. I could run, but I couldn't hide.

The blackout was sudden. I had never been in a city of complete darkness. It's black in the way that the desert is black, but blacker still because the buildings block out stars, the moon and any sense of perspective.

The public square was still a hive of activity like in all Chi-nese towns on Friday nights; shadows of a hundred people still dancing.

Fluorescent and glowing toys came out, hula hoops, battery-lit shoes, glow sticks. The interiors of shops along the main road started bouncing with candlelight. It was a small but telling exam-ple of a recurring problem during Chinese summers. The year before, China's second-largest grid operator, Southern Power Grid Company, which covered this area, had predicted a massive power shortfall of 7.8 gigawatts. That's about the same as the total generat-ing capacity of wind power in America, which can produce enough electricity on a typical day to power over 2.5 million homes. Black-outs and brownouts were frequent, and the village here seemed well prepared.

On one of the main bridges across the tributary I watched apart-ment windows hover like square moons in the otherwise inky sky. The buildings were built right up to the water's edge. Light doubled back and forth between building and water.

A lone man began to play a Chinese flute from his long, thin boat on the river, crystal-clear tones cutting the night air, finding the city's harmonics. His lamp shed a single yellow frame.

Then. *What's that smell?*

An arc of light from a car illuminated the fact that I was standing next to the town's waste dump. Gross. I went back to the hotel, lit a candle and sweated out a night without air-conditioning.

China encourages foreigners to enter Tibet from the north. At the time of writing, the new Beijing-Lhasa railway line was still closed to foreigners, though it was taking its large daily freight of Chinese into Tibet.

The authorities favour large, high-rolling tour groups, led by Chinese tour guides well-versed in communist propaganda. The Chinese government forbids independent travel. Get caught, and you're fined and told to leave. Keen to see a less-filtered Tibet, I opened Tibet's southern back door through Yunnan, a heavily monitored route, where only certified operators run four-wheel-drive tours.

After days of paper shuffling to get my alien travel permit rubber-stamped by five government departments, I had a Tibetan guide, a Pajero to tackle the mountain passes (which climb over 5,000 metres above sea level, twice as high as Australia's tallest peak), and seven days to drive overland to Lhasa.

After coughing up that much cash, I was set for Tibet to choke me with majesty, but the Tibet I found was heavily controlled. The Tibet I was permitted to see was thoroughly Chinese, down to its internet-gaming parlours and thumping Lhasa clubs. Thuptan (or Tuppy, my nickname for him), was my 26-year-old guide, himself a fan of Chinese modernisation. He wore a spectrum-blue t-shirt emblazoned with 'Nirvana' – the band, not the destination – Michael Jordan-era hightops, and walked like a breakdancer.

'Bome,' he told me, 'is the second-best town on the way to Lhasa.' My notion of best was a town that boasted untainted Tibetan culture. His notion of best was a town with electricity, TV and Western toilets.

Lhasa only heightened my concerns. In the glorious Potala Palace, a monk offered me snuff tobacco from a small tin. Monks here are not allowed to wear their robes, I'm told. 'Have you seen him?' he asked, referring to the Dalai Lama. Of course, I said, on TV. His eyes became moist, shaking his prayer beads. The monk saw the Dalai Lama once as a boy, but can't remember now, it was too long ago.

Facing the Potala Palace, like a big middle finger sticking out of the People's Square, stands the Chinese monument to liberation. It's a reminder of occupation. Not that there are many Tibetans left to remind: Tibetans now only make up one-third of the population, and own even less of the businesses.

On the roof of the magical Jokhang Temple, the centre of a pilgrim whirlpool, Jackbo, a 22-year-old monk studying English, whispered, 'I feel Tibetan culture become weaker and weaker.' There's no Tibetan taught in schools, he said, only Mandarin, and development has threatened the environment. Jackbo tells me none of the money from the temple's entrance fee will go to Tibetans. In the smaller, more idiosyncratic Ramoche temple, I asked why there are no pictures of the Dalai Lama where there would normally be a shrine. I knew the answer, but wanted his opinion. 'The Chinese government will attack,' Jackbo responded in his anxious, courteous English.

I walked around Ranwu Hai between Paksho and Bome, the largest lake in southeast Tibet, at 3,800 metres above sea level. I sat at its edges on the cushion grass, meditating under the high sky. Earlier that day I had drunk salty yak-butter tea with a nomadic family in yak-skinned tents, surrounded by eight snotty and inquisitive children. I had seen the meeting point of the three great rivers, the Mekong, the Salween and the Yellow.

But the memory that sticks the most is of the Potala Palace's caretaker monk, his eyes wet with affection, jarring with Tuppy's insistence on a unified Chinese culture.

'You ask a lot of questions,' Tuppy said one day, an odd thing for a guide to have a problem with.

'I'm curious.'

'Well. I'm Chinese. Chinese and Tibetan are the same. There used to be fifty-five minorities in China. We are the fifty-sixth.'

I woke to the smell of stoked camel dung and the gurgle of water poured on something hot. Smoky light from the yurt's opening fell across sleeping bodies. The young wife in a pink headscarf and tatty hosiery carried lake water to begin steaming breakfast buns. K'chuk, the puppy tethered outside, barked at a motorcycle gunning then humming ever distantly to the highway, perhaps to meet the morning buses with offers of accommodation or bike rides to the glacier.

The night had not been too cold in this felty womb, pinned under heavy blankets. Winds whistled through the yurt's seams like ancient language.

I slept deeply and dreamed of distant Beijing between K'chuk's barking fits. He was a golden dog of some pristine herding breed with bright eyes and white teeth. Released from his rope in the morning hours, I heard the protests of goats and sheep and a camel's long mournful moo. K'chuk was chasing them with malicious innocence.

I liked the hard sleeping-mat and the otherworldly darkness of the yurt, and reluctantly peeled back my layers, pulled on a jumper and peeked outside. Such remote beauty amazed me. Or perhaps it was my shortness of breath at this 3,500-metre altitude, mistaken for an immense, inspiring moment.

The brightening morning exposed rattish plains, and the surreal rise of the Pamirs, snow-capped and shedding clouds like science experiments, even in July. Muztagh Ata, the icy 7,500-metre peak, dominated the entire range.

Karakul Lake was a thin blue gash across the plain, flanked by grass. Goat herds grazed there. Several brightly clothed, toothless women were doing their laundry at the lake's edge. Directly above, five or six weather systems fretted about a giant arch of sky. There, a single grey swarm of rain bent its short lifespan over one mountain before vanishing. A rainbow lost its absurd colour from another low cloud. The sky in other corners was deep and blue.

I had the afternoon to myself. And in that solitude, in the kind of landscape that makes me shy, I sat and read, feeling very much like I was on the brink of China.

I was in China's most westerly corner, on the edge of Xinjiang, the frontier. This place occupied the mythic bounds of my imagination; I was dreaming of overlords, savages and traders – great allegories for the story of globalisation. I thought this desert might provide a final and poetic counterpoint to Beijing.

This autonomous Muslim region comprises a sixth of China's landmass and shares borders with eight countries: the '-stans', plus Russia, Mongolia and the Indian-administered bits of Kashmir. Past Tashkurgan, another southern minority prefecture (here Chinese characters compete awkwardly with the lavish flow of Arabic), is the passage into Pakistan. At nearly 4,700 metres, Khunjareb Pass is the world's highest paved pass. North, the other direction, is the pass into Kazakhstan.

Karakul Lake is in the Kizilsu Kyrgyz prefecture. Kizilsu means 'red water' in the local language, perhaps a reference to the sandstone-tinged streams before I passed Sand Mountain, which wears its sand like tailored velvet above wet plains. The area is mainly populated by Muslim Uyghur and Kyrgyz groups, ethnically distinct from the Han Chinese that make up a small but powerful percentage.

I was now on the furthest edge of China's territory, but in this frontier land of China, borders are zones for contact and control. The real intention is cultural gentrification. The yurt lake itself is only a few hours from Kashgar, that famed 2,000-year-old chimera of cultures that was once a hub on the Silk Route, and is now an outlandish experiment in Chinese domination. Mao's statue in Kashgar's People's Square is said to be China's tallest, nearly twenty-five metres high on a spotlit platform, and his distant eyes seem to stare all the way to Tiananmen.

The city's other meeting place, around the Id Kah mosque built in 1442, is more welcoming with its local markets, Hotan jade, bejewelled knives, and kids slurping ice drinks watching television. And yet, here in China's biggest mosque, a plaque declares, 'The Chinese government always pays special attention to the other, historical cultures of ethnic groups, and all ethnic groups welcome the Party's religious policy . . . All ethnic groups live in friendship together here.' In 2001, the mosque came under the administration that looks after cultural relics, though it is not a relic. China's biggest congregation of Muslims, 10,000 worshippers, gather here every Friday.

The minarets of mosques provide stunning views across the crowded mudbrick old town, which is smoky with grills and red hot tandoors producing blistered naan bread. The dusty alleys in Kashgar are from dreams. But outside the old town there are strip malls and fast-food chains and bars pumping pop. Like everywhere in China, desire has dollar signs.

A China with a fast metabolism for raw energy is filling the desert with money. The region has one-third of China's total gas reserves, one-quarter of its oil, and two-fifths of its coal. All is to be dug up and pumped east. Beyond the borders, the Ataru Alashankuo oil pipeline now links Kazakhstan and Xinjiang and will eventually extend to the Caspian Sea. When it opened in 2006, it was the first time foreign oil flowed directly into China. A year on, it was delivering 100,000 barrels a day. In Beijing parlance, it's called 'Develop the West', a series of policies that pour money into the rural west, with Xinjiang – meaning 'new dominion' in Chinese – being the main recipient.

There's a palpable tension between the Han, the immigrants, those heading west for profit and new lives, and the local population of Muslims, who can have blue eyes and fairer hair, angular faces with grave expressions. The government has heavily suppressed

Uyghur culture and the idea of an independent state. September 11 and the US-led War on Terror gave Beijing an excuse to call separatists 'terrorists' and further clamp down on activity.

The military and police presence here is heavy; the desert is randomly measured by sandblasted military compounds, government buildings and, in the same vein, China Mobile towers. In the middle of the Taklamakan desert – a brilliant exposure of sand-tanned nothingness, empty as the sea – modern China gives me full bars of mobile-phone coverage.

Beijing is so close I can smell its breath and feel its heat on my cheek.

Three years ago, the government tourism authority took over this area next to the yurt lake, erected a China Mobile tower, built some fake concrete yurts, and started to charge an entrance fee of 50 kuai (£4), something my host Sadik shielded me from, explaining that I was a student. 'They never help us,' says Sadik of the police. 'Whenever they see foreigners, they come to the yurts to harass us.'

Sadik is 25 but looks well into his 30s. His skin is dark and creased from the sun, his teeth are rotten. Yet he has a youthful camaraderie and sprawls about the yurt, chatting and drinking tea. Sadik and Buer'jia, his wife of two and a half years, erect this yurt in May for the summer months until October when tourism falls off. He's been doing this for several years. While he scouts for yurt guests in the summer, friends from a nearby village tend his flock of sixty sheep. In the fierce winter months he withdraws to his small apartment two kilometres away to sell sheep and cultivate a new flock, and his friends return to village jobs like teaching.

Sadik is a Chinese citizen. His family has always lived in this area. His wife's mother looks after their boy, aged eighteen months, in the village so the young couple can be free to engage in the fledgling industry that the highway has pulled into the region. They miss their child, and visit him once a week. Despite all their efforts, the money is not enough to get them through the winter.

To augment what most certainly cannot be called income, Buer'jia makes hand-sewn blankets and rugs.

Inside the yurt, we were a world away from the threats of a changing China. A small tape player had one cassette permanently rusted to its insides. The gas oven's lower drawers stored bread and vegetables. Bric-a-brac was suspended from the yurt's skeletal beams – sunglasses, a photo album, tools with no express purpose, cooking implements. The small central stove burned a simple heat all day.

'Five years is the longest we will be here,' Sadik says. 'It definitely will change. I don't know when but it will. Whenever someone realises how many people come here, a company, either govern-ment-run, or privately run, will come and take it over and kick us out.'

With each adventurer and passer-by, a gust of this inevitability blows through this land. But Sadik seems neither fazed nor emo-tional about this.

He shrugs. 'This is our place', he says. 'It's our country.'

As I flagged down a bus, clouds delivered a spray of rain, which made Karakul Lake shimmer briefly before resuming its stubborn glare of the western sun.

CHAPTER 25
BEIJING BY NUMBERS

In a few days' time I will leave Beijing. The day will be, as Jenny might say, mad as an arse full of bats.

On the same day I leave, Beijing will welcome around 260 new lives, perhaps at one of the city's eighteen specialised maternity care hospitals. Or at some of the other 519 hospitals in the capital. One of Beijing's nearly 40,000 certified doctors will cut an umbilical cord and hear the screams of Beijing's newest residents add to the city's cries.

Friends and family will be notified on some of the 4.1 million mobile phone calls made that day on Beijing's cellular networks. Making a call will be easy since nearly everyone owns a mobile phone – a reported 12.5 million handsets in Beijing alone. If they don't, it will be simple to buy one because 250,000 extra mobile phones will be available for purchase.

Relatives in another province or living abroad may receive news of a baby's birth via one of the 1.7 million letters posted at one of the capital's thousands of postboxes.

Elsewhere in the municipality, on the day I leave more than fifteen million people will wake up in their apartments of 50 square metres each and prepare to join their neighbours on the streets. Some of this traffic will travel on Beijing's 1,125 kilometres of railway lines. If it's an average day, 68,000 will disembark from Beijing's main railway station in the centre of the city.

For the 7.5 million registered as employed in Beijing it's just another day at the office. The average worker will make 48.4 kuai (£3.95) the day I leave and will spend three-quarters of it, mainly on living costs.

Police will attend seventeen major road accidents and nineteen people will be ferried off to hospital as a result. Only four Beijingers will die in that day's traffic.

There will be fires in twenty-three locations on the day I leave, each hopefully answered by one of the city's 381 fire trucks.

For every 100 households in Beijing, there are 206 bikes. If you are one of nearly 860,000 secondary school students, you might ride one of these bikes to school at one of the city's 3,782 schools (including primary schools).

The 672,000 registered construction workers will join myriad unregistered ones on an astonishing number of construction sites (Xinhua news agency says there are 8,000 ongoing sites, 30% of which don't meet regulations on pollution).

Love will be celebrated at 256 weddings – that's down from a similar day last year. Conversely, sixty-six couples will divorce, up from a similar day last year.

There will be sadness in the city today too: 216 people will die in Beijing, at an average age of seventy-six.

While Beijing's human theatre performs outside, I will use numbers to get through the process of leaving. I will pack into two large China Post boxes the accumulation of twelve months: thirteen jumpers, four pair of trousers, six t-shirts, five collared shirts, two sets of thermal underwear, four hats and three scarves, a suit jacket, two ties, two belts, one blanket, and a big winter jacket. Seven books are making the cut to the next stage of my life, along with thirteen CDs packed into one CD wallet. A map, a guidebook, summer Ts, shorts and a pair of jeans, an iPod and a laptop are coming with me.

I've been through two apartments and two bikes, a stack of mosquito coils, thousands of kuai in taxi rides, kilolitres of Tsingtao and a string of crushes. I will take in my heart a bounty of friendships: Jenny, Yoni, Wang Xiaoke, Wang Miao, Jack and Stephen, among many more.

Beijing will open its doors the day I leave. The city will welcome 9,945 new international tourists and 228 of these will be Australian, a number up 130% from the same day last year.

They can stay at one of Beijing's 594 hotels and take a trip to one of the city's thirty-four museums, read up on culture in one of the twenty-six public libraries, or see one of the small number of films presented in China on a screen at one of its 160 cinemas.

International tourism, however, will be dwarfed by domestic tourism the day I leave. Nearly 350,000 Chinese tourists will descend on Beijing, and contribute towards an annual 356 million kuai (£29 million) tourism-spending spree in the capital.

The day I leave the city I will be one of nearly 133,000 passengers to pass through Beijing Capital Airport, the world's ninth busiest. I will walk through the doors and turn my back on the city. But only for a time.

CHAPTER 26

SEASONAL CHANGE

There was a dilapidated stretch of the Great Wall at Huang Hua ('Yellow Flower'), where my flatmate Yoni knew a man with a courtyard house we could rent for a night of unhinged celebration; a last chance to get away from the maddening crowds and find breathable air before I left Beijing.

To get to Huang Hua we rented a minivan from Dongzhimen bus stop, the hub of the new airport line being built for the coming Olympics, where men shopped cheap rides to lesser-known sections of the Great Wall. With the compulsory ritual of haggling, laughing and mock-anger fulfilled, we piled in – me, Yoni and several other expat friends – for the two-hour drive north.

Beijing's northern expanse was trapped in the present participle, somewhere between being and becoming. Around the railway line's various half-built stations, each a tangle of beams and exposed concrete staircases, satellite cities defied reason in both size and number. Where wheat crops once grew alongside the road, plantations of Spanish condominiums now thrived like introduced species without any natural competition. These bright white buildings didn't exist last winter when we first made this trip to Huang Hua – a bizarre simulacrum of American suburbia, these luxury dwellings. Bound by wide streets, newly planted trees, lamp-posts and picket fences, they were Chinese middle-class fantasies made concrete.

Huang Hua was a peaceful respite. In winter, trees here were bare, the mountains deserted of green and the air pale, thin and dry. In summer, the valley was hot and lush, almost tropical. The courtyard house was located in a village that was in a state of flux: piles of blond building bricks were stacked ready to be cobbled into houses that would eventually, Yoni thought, form the backbone of a tourist town at some stage. For now, it was one of his better-kept secrets.

The small houses were dotted around a dammed river, into which the village emptied garbage and waste. Dogs and chickens picked through the muck at the side of the dam and up the hill, and men in handmade straw hats pulled donkeys laden with cut wood and other commodities. Kids approached and rumbled, teeth bared in gappy smiles. What was not over-grown by pine trees and grasses was yellow exposed earth. A graffitied factory with a crumbling chimney stack and smashed windows was deserted. A dark ping-pong hall down the road hosted only a handful of youths.

Inside the courtyard was a collector's indiscriminate horde of trash and treasure: rusty wheels, hanging skins, lanterns, petrol tanks, pots, pans, chairs. Moving inside further still, into the rooms, was like opening the tomb of a deranged dilettante. Creepy dolls, a transistor radio, endless bits and pieces of memorabilia. Framed photographs.

We sat on the Great Wall, untroubled by bottled-water sellers and prayer-bead hawkers, and with no air-conditioned coaches to interrupt the view. The smokers rolled long and smelly joints. Most of the wall here had surrendered to nature long ago; in parts, China's most recognisable icon was reduced to a mere suggestion, a memory. But in other sections it defied time, marching high on the ridges.

This was where I sat later, having absented myself from the group for a time in the evening. Being so high made me think of Beijing's flatness, its burrows and haunts, its partitioned world. It felt like waking from sleep.

In the quiet, I remembered that first time I had set eyes upon

the battlements of the Great Wall a year ago; I felt awed and surprised by the architectural feat, and by the accompanying rave. I had
kept a clipping of the *China Daily* from the next day. The paper was
outraged that youngsters had gathered 'for vigorous dance, strong
music and wine'. Another report called it an orgy of sex and drugs,
and published a picture of someone lending literal meaning to 'pissing up against the wall'. 'They are simply blaspheming our national
symbol,' Dong Yaohui of the China Great Wall Association complained to the UK's *Telegraph*. What they didn't write about was
what I had seen that night: swirls of globalisation, sexuality and
attitude wrapping around a China I would grow to love.

I positioned myself on the wall to look back towards Beijing.
Insect noise surged in the undergrowth. My palms felt the day's
heat trapped in the broken bits of brick, some covered in lichen,
some weathered smooth. Grass grew up though the cracks and
itched my legs. Light, filtered by wood smoke, was hot on my neck,
and I turned to squint into that hazy circle of the Chinese sun, a sun
found nowhere else in the world.

The silence was conducive to reflection. I felt ambivalent about
the understanding of China I'd acquired in twelve short months.
China was many things I aspired to be myself: an optimist, sincerely
accommodating of change. But there lingered questions of freedom
and how to deal with the past. While it seemed clear that China
wanted to drop the cultural suitcases at the bottom of the stairs and
climb up into the future without them, would that forfeit something
of the intellectual and cultural evolution that must accompany last-
ing economic success?

More than anything, I longed for China to reward its young artists and thinkers like Hao for wanting their country to be better.
They might express this love through ideas rather than blind loyalty, but my feeling was that their aim was diversity rather than
dissent.

The sun dropped behind the last westerly mountain; a dynamic
shift. The air cooled and the trees adopted an almost purple hue. Vil-

lage lights budded below. I slapped a mosquito on my forearm. I had found core strength because of Beijing. It was hard to know whether I would be this white or tired if I had stayed in Sydney, whether I would have had these rings under my eyes. My face had changed; I looked and felt older. Because of Beijing, I had my mandate for adulthood.

I sat and watched the old defences trace away, like a fault-line buckled by the rub of tectonic plates. The wall almost looked like it had grown out of the earth.

In the dusk, I picked a path down the steep slope and entered the village, lured by the smell of seared meat and the bangs and sizzles of cooking. I pushed open the wooden doors to join the music and celebrations inside the courtyard, where empty bottles were already accumulating on the windowsill.

Here the stars could battle Beijing's glow, and they added their light to the courtyard's candles. In the blurry hours after midnight, our voices raised in farewell echoed across the valley. By morning, all that remained of Beijing's roar was a ringing in my ears.

RESOURCES

Useful words

baijiu A clear and powerful spirit distilled from rice or other grains – it tastes like it's been filtered through a share-house mattress.

chai Meaning 'demolition', this is the symbol spray-painted on buildings slated for the wrecking ball.

chuanr Skewer of grilled meat, popular as a street-food snack.

gaokou Three-day national university-entrance exams.

Han The majority of the Chinese population.

hong bao Red envelopes stuffed with money and given as gifts on special occasions and during holidays, especially to mark Chinese New Year.

hukao Official work and residency permit, increasingly irrelevant as the job market opens.

hutong Used to refer to the alleyways that once criss-crossed Beijing, and to the neighbourhoods they create.

jian bing Egg pancake.

jiaozi Dumpling.

kuai Common term for yuan, the main Chinese unit of currency.

lala Lesbian.

laoban A male boss.

mao Common term for small change (10 mao = 1 kuai).

shuai Good-looking, suave.

si he yuan Traditional courtyard house.

tongzhi Gay.

Blogs

www.danwei.org
Critical and entertaining, Danwei is a daily survey of Chinese media by long-term expats. Danwei also hosts podcasts and videos.

www.zonaeuropa.com
EastSouthWestNorth is an index of translations of articles posted by China's most influential, or infamous, writers. It also links to articles in both Chinese and English, and comments on the often-erroneous coverage of China in the West. It's both exhaustive and exhausting to look through – and, for his efforts, Roland Soong, the blog's Hong Kong-based creator, receives nearly 42,000 hits a day.

www.beijingorbust.blogspot.com
Humble but blistering, Beijing or Bust is Hao Wu's personal blog about China's contradictions.

Books

Tongzhi: Politics of Same-Sex Eroticism in Chinese Societies, Chou Wah-Shan (Hawthorn Press, New York). An academic history of gay and lesbian life in China and Taiwan.

Remaking Beijing: Tiananmen Square and the Creation of a Political Space, Wu Hung (University of Chicago Press, Chicago). A beautifully illustrated history of Beijing's urban landscape, including responses to Tiananmen Square by contemporary Chinese artists. Art historian Wu Hung also recounts his personal journeys through the streets of Beijing.

The Insider's Guide to Beijing, edited by Adam Pillsbury (China Intercontinental Press, Beijing). Simply put, this is the expat's Bible: how to bargain, where to find the best massage, medical care, or maid. Even better are the lists of restaurants, galleries and attractions with names given in Chinese characters and pinyin, as well as English.

Music

Cut Off! Rebuilding the Rights of Statues. Dirty post punk and rock.

Secret Mission, Wednesday's Trip. Earnest trip-hop with plenty of acoustic strumming to accompany sweet female vocals.

Mental Imagery, Dead J Ambient. Glitch and electronic beats, warm and sometimes fuzzy with spacious loops.

Beijing Dream, Thin Man. Guitar rock.

Film

Dong Gong Xi Gong (East Palace, West Palace), directed by Yuan Zhang (1996). Banned in China, this is the mainland's first gay film. A young writer A-lan hangs out in the Forbidden City gardens. At night he waits for sex in the pagodas. When one police officer singles him out for abuse, A-lan is taken in as a 'hooligan' and suffers a night-long interrogation laced with danger and eroticism. The film's point is that 'hooliganism' is both created by authority and perpetuated by it.

2046, directed by Wong Kar Wai (2004). A meditation on memory and loss, this sumptuous film is alternately set in 1960s Hong Kong and a parallel techno-world called 2046, complete with sexy, inscrutable androids.

ACKNOWLEDGEMENTS

For Chinese-language help, my thanks go to Elena Bresciani, Tamsin Westley and Kevin Hou. My super thanks to Nisly Lin, for her quick and always-lovely translations. Additional reporting and interviews in Chapter Seven, '*Niu Bi*', were conducted by Hao Wu and Changying Liu.

For English-language help and expert guidance, I'm awed by Melanie Ostell. She's got the skills and knows how to use them. Alison Cowan's touch can be felt everywhere in this work; and the design talents of Daniel New, Claire Wilson and Evi O have brought it to life. Publisher Julie Gibbs has been a faithful and thoughtful custodian throughout. To my agent Fran Moore, thanks for your support. You're wonderful.

To my travel partners – in particular Sophie Wiesner, Brian Chang and Jennifer Yau – I will cherish the sleeper bus (China's most vociferous version of civil society), *baijiu* binges and high-altitude hitching.

Jenny and Yoni, my soul mates, this would not have been possible without your laughter, love and weight training.

The heart of this book was cared for from beginning to end by my dear friend David Berthold, who over two years read every word and listened to a million more, because he wanted to. Thanks are not enough.

Lastly to Mum, Dad and Marc, for the love and everything else.